"When you recover or
discover something
that nourishes your
soul and brings joy,
care enough about
yourself to make room
for it in your life."
~ Jean Shinoda Bolen

Thorn & Bloom Magazine 04: Radical Joy We Cultivate

Edited by Kirsty Anne Richards

ISBN: 979-8-9931229-3-9

Published by:
redrosethorns Ltd. Liability Co. (USA)
Also operating as redrosethorns Ltd. (UK)
www.redrosethorns.com

Table of Contents

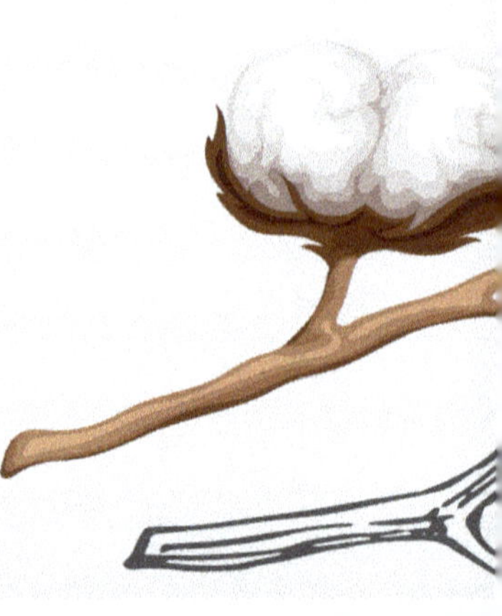

redrosethorns press

redrosethorns journal

Our core publication, *redrosethorns journal*, is dedicated to exploring themes of mental health, self-care, gender and sexuality, and empowerment. Through the literature we publish, we aim not only to raise awareness of these topics but also to educate, inspire, and empower our readers.

As an online journal, redrosethorns features diverse literary works across all genres and styles, released monthly. To ensure accessibility, all pieces are free to read, and our subscribers receive a featured piece each week, fostering ongoing conversations and engagement.

Thorn & Bloom Magazines

Thorn & Bloom is a quarterly publication exploring self-care as a radical act of resilience and liberation. We launched with a debut issue in March 2025 that sparked conversations on socialisation, self-awareness, and critical thinking. Our second edition, *Breaking the Cycle*, published in June 2025, built on this foundation by examining how we break away from the narratives that harm us. Followed by our third edition, *The Splinters We Carry*, which focused on the issues, both personal and political, that cause us harm. Each edition is filled with curated essays, poetry, and reflections on reclaiming autonomy through intentional practice. The magazine is dedicated to the principle that true self-care begins with knowing oneself — a journey that requires confronting the forces that keep us from fulfilment, and incorporating aspects in our lives that complement our authentic selves.

redrosethorns magazines

Our publishing journey began with a print literary magazine – *redrosethorns magazine 01: community/connection* - followed by two more editions - *redrosethorns magazine 02: home/belonging* and *redrosethorns magazine 03: rebellion/conformity* – in an annual series. Each issue was centred around a theme, reflecting both the growth of our platform and the essential conversations needed to foster positive mental health.

After three years, we decided to complete the series as a trilogy, allowing us to shift our focus toward expanding other publications and creating more events that bring these themes to life.

Thorn & Bloom

EDITORIAL DIRECTOR

Kirsty Anne Richards

ABOUT THIS MAGAZINE

For our fourth edition, we dive into the heart of what makes life feel vibrant, soft, and truly our own, and shift our gaze to the lighter, loving side of liberation. This issue champions the belief that self-care is not just a healing balm for wounds, but the daily practice of filling your cup with pure, unadulterated joy. *Radical Joy We Cultivate* is a rebellious act to choose play over productivity, to prioritise pleasure, and to nurture the moments that make your soul spark. The personal rituals that return us to ourselves not to be more productive, but to be more present, free, and authentically us.

LANGUAGE DISCLAIMER

Our publications offer literature from a diverse community found within our global society. To honour the voices of our authors, we have deliberately kept various English dialects found within each persons work and their respective spellings.

ABOUT REDROSETHORNS

redrosethorns is an educational publication company, specialising in literature centred around mental health, self-care, gender & sexuality, and empowerment. Founded on feminist principles, we believe that through art and literature, we can foster empathy and connection to empower each other to live our authentic selves, while building a society that is inclusive and accepting of all diversities.

FROM THE EDITOR

Kirsty Anne Richards is the founder and editorial director of redrosethorns Ltd. Liability Co. (USA) / redrosethorns Ltd. (UK). With a background in psychology, gender/sexuality, and feminism, she is deeply committed to examining the complexities of identity, empowerment, and well-being. Through her work, she strives to create spaces for meaningful dialogue, challenging conventional narratives and encouraging others to cultivate self-worth beyond societal expectations.

An avid reader, Kirsty Anne embraces literature as a vital part of her self-care practice, weaving its lessons into her daily life. She is passionate about the arts and finds joy in travelling, dancing, and writing. She currently lives in London.

Kirsty Anne

EDITORIAL DIRECTOR

As the year reaches its end, we chose to focus on a positive theme to propel us forward into a new year, a new chapter, and to remind ourselves of the things that make life so worthwhile. When thinking of pleasure, it is not merely that it brings us joy and happiness, but that it is the antithesis of all the stress, hardships, and horror we experience in life. Our self-care practice is, in large part, an active engagement to learn more about our inner selves and to create a life that authentically represents who we are at our core. This comes with recognising what influenced our thoughts and behaviours, and how we can learn to break free from the shackles that keep us stuck, stagnant, or from expressing our inner beings. But it is also a practice of incorporating things that contribute to our overall happiness.

Joy seemed the apt subject to focus this edition of *Thorn & Bloom*, to remind ourselves that there is so much in life to be grateful for and to look forward to. Ensuring that we prioritise the things we love is not only so that we can strive toward overall well-being or fulfilment, but also to reflect who we are to others. Our hobbies, routines, the people and aspects of life we love, all tell a story of who we are and invite others to share our lives together. Because in doing the things we enjoy, we find parts of ourselves and a connection with others.

Reading all the submissions that came in illuminated the beauty in human beings and reminded me of how much more life there is to explore. Not just in the activities one could pursue, but in the things we often dismiss or take for granted that are right there in the spaces we occupy. I have a beautiful view of London, and see the sun rise and set each day from my flat. Birds fly past my windows, and the cool breeze in the summer soothes my overheated skin. But also, the candle burning in the evening brings a sweet scent and calming feeling at the end of a long day. All the little things around us can easily invite serenity and pleasure into our everyday lives. The stories shared in these pages bring awareness to the multitude of joy there is in life. Sometimes, in challenging ourselves with a new adventure, sometimes basking in the simple pleasures, and sometimes in the kindness from strangers.

Whatever joy may look like to you, know that it is more than an act of self-care; it is a rebellious intention to refuse to adhere to those who wish to take it away. Finding and focusing on the joys in our lives is a radical act of intentional liberation that no one can take away, no one can replicate, and no one can mould to suit their needs. It is the one thing that is entirely our own and something we can share with others.

Life is filled with ups and downs, but what keeps us grounded, and maybe even sane, is to come back to the things and people we love to remind us that there is always so much more to look forward to. If there is one takeaway I can offer you as you peruse these stories, it is to look up and look around when life brings you down, and know that you are not alone, you are loved, and your life is overflowing with more wondrous pleasures than you can ever imagine. Your only job is to find it.

"The greatest pleasure in life is doing what people say you cannot do."

~ Walter Bagehot

If we are what we love

by Carolyn Chilton Casas

then I am soft mornings
in solitude, no sounds
except the sincerity of birdsong,
a book or pad on my lap,
hot cup of *café de olla* at my side.
I am the sunny hours to come
free from my list's must-be-dones,
brisk walk on the beach,
true connection with a friend
like the frog calling to me now.
Tender shades of yellow, blue, and green.
I crave a simple life, little fuss,
no clutter, few dire needs,
priorities set to whatever brings
laughter and awe.
Time for the lightness of being
that arises from creating
something I can share
with the world I so love.

"It's not what you look at, it's what you see."
– Thoreau

"I am the monarch of all I survey."
– Cowper

Walking out of my house in Wellfleet, I cross the street and follow a sandy horse-trail that weaves through my neighbor's place. Oak and maple trees create a canopy just over my head–a cool tunnel even in the middle of the summer. Bearberry, sheep laurel and scrub oak brush my ankles as I walk.

In a little less than a mile, the trail opens onto Cahoon Hollow, a narrow road that snakes down to dunes and the National Seashore. Across the road is Great Pond, formed by the last glacier when it retreated 12,000 years ago. Great Pond is about a third of a mile across and almost perfectly round. There's a wooden stairway down to the water and a narrow beach of white sand at the bottom of the stairs. The water is cool in May and June, but it warms up in the summer and stays in the 70s until October. The bottom of the pond is sandy, and the water is clear and pure, so when you swim, you can see the sand until you are well over your head.

During the summer, my wife and I swim here or in one of the other ponds nearby almost every day. If you follow the fire road that runs alongside Great Pond for half a mile, you'll come to Dyer Pond; its claim to fame is a rope swing suspended from a tree. If you keep going, you'll soon get to Long Pond—a favorite of families with its beach and parking. All the ponds are technically lakes because they have little vegetation growing in them; all of them are beautiful, especially at the end of the day when the light filters through the pines and glimmers off the scrub oak leaves to prance along the water.

When it gets hot, we head to the beach. There are beaches on both sides of the cape. On the Outer Banks, the harbor and the ocean are only a couple of miles apart. The beaches on the harbor side are family-friendly with small waves and easy access. Since they face west, they are a great place to watch the sunset. But the best beaches are on the ocean side.

About a mile east on Cahoon Hollow from Great Pond, the road intersects with Ocean View Drive. If you go straight across, you plunge downhill to Cahoon Hollow beach, where the Beachcomber Bar sits atop a plateau of sand, and a steep trail cuts down the dunes to the shore. Cahoon Hollow draws the crowds, but the best, most spectacular beach is about a mile north.

White Crest Beach sits at the bottom of 75-foot dunes. Each year, a new trail has to be carved by beachgoers since the ocean and wind wash and blow the trail away during the winter. The trail cuts diagonally down to the beach. It's an easy lope down but a challenging climb back up. At its base is an expanse of white and ochre sand where you can watch the ocean roll in on two to four-foot waves.

For the last few summers, seals have been trolling by, and there have been a few Great White shark sightings.

A number of houses that sit precariously atop the cliffs on Ocean View have been moved back away from the dunes in the past twenty-five years. Last year, the Beachcomber lost half its shore-side parking lot to winter storms.

The ocean is usually cold. Stay in long, and the numbness works its way up from your toes. It's refreshing, though, when the temperature gets into the 80s. It can be rough with an undertow, but at low tide it's great for body surfing, boogie boarding and for surfers skilled enough to pop up and ride the fast-breaking waves diagonally. It never gets crowded at White Crest. There's plenty of room to set up horseshoes or play whiffle-ball or tag football.

The roads in Wellfleet are narrow and hilly, so the Outer Banks is a spectacular place to ride a bike, although drivers of cars need to be patient. They usually are. I like to take a ten-mile route that circles Great Pond to Long Pond and up Gross Hill to Ocean View past Gull Pond. You can also follow the harbor out Chequessett Road on rolling hills that pass beautiful houses that perch on the hill and peer out at the bay.

If it's not too hot, and my knees are up to it, I like to jog on the trails that run through the woods past the ponds to Long Pond Road, up the big hill and then along the ocean and back through the woods to my house. There I'll take an outdoor shower followed by a beer, fresh fish on the grill and dinner on the deck. I keep the feeders full and watch blue jays, cardinals, rock doves, and chickadees fly in for free food. In June, bluebirds and Baltimore Orioles stop by. If we're lucky, hummingbirds helicopter in to sip sugar water.

What happens when you're immersed in such a beautiful environment is that time begins to change its shape. The straight line of the digital clock fades into the background of trail walks and swims in crystal clear water and late-afternoon light flashing through trees while shadows crawl across ponds. Eventually, you begin to feel as if you are part of the natural world and that world exudes a certain power. Part of that power everyone recognizes as reducing stress, allowing you to relax, but it goes beyond that. It's effortlessly rewarding. You don't have to work at it; you can just accept it as a gift. That gift is uplifting in a way that has nothing to do with organized religion but is intimately tied to spirituality.

I imagine this is what I'll miss when I'm no longer here—on earth, I mean. But I can live with that as long as I know it will be here for those who follow after I'm gone.

***

Dalliance
by Heather Holliger

We had developed a habit of walking trails together. You sprinted ahead, pausing to explore anything with an interesting scent. I didn't know why certain odors intrigued you more than others, but I did know that the more something stunk—a rotting apple, a brackish puddle, excrement of any kind—the more it captivated you. Because of your heightened sense of smell—you have millions more scent receptors that humans do—you likely knew where I was even if you couldn't see me, and yet, you kept me in view, somehow never venturing outside my own line of sight. Every so often, you'd turn in my direction and make eye contact, as if seeking some kind of reassurance. As long as I didn't call your name, or gesture for your return, you'd canter along ahead of me, attuned to whatever sweetness or rank might be awaiting your discovery. Long-legged, but short in stature, not quite as tall as my knees, with your white, tan-spotted fur, your round, copper-brushed ears and white-tipped tail, you could have been mistaken for a miniature, albeit out-of-place deer.

Veering off our usual path, we found an unmowed field with goal posts at each end, what I surmised must once have been a soccer field. At first, you seemed to hesitate. Perhaps you had grown accustomed to human-made paths, trails through the woods and sidewalks in the city. In contrast, here was an expanse of green, something you probably hadn't encountered, at least not off leash, since I adopted you from the shelter. You tentatively began to explore your surroundings, sniffing at the air, burying your nose in purple

clover, ambling to-and-fro in some overgrown, leafy vegetation, your tiny paw prints momentarily visible in still wet grass.

I had turned to admire something, though I don't remember what, perhaps one of the gnarled old oak trees, or a patch of wildflowers. But it must not have been of consequence. When I looked around, what I saw took my breath away. A yellow butterfly held you in rapt attention, and you appeared to be engaged in a game of chase. I'd watched you run after squirrels and rabbits, never actually catching up with them. While I knew it was likely instinct for you to hunt small animals, when on occasion you happened upon a dead baby bird or some other maimed living thing, you'd only ever managed to pick it up in your mouth and walk around with it like a prize. Inevitably, you grew tired of it, abandoned it like a rag doll, unscathed.

Unlike a squirrel, moving in the grass along a horizontal path in our backyard, the butterfly moved in grand circles, in arcs. She could close her wings, make herself nearly invisible, and then spring to life in a burst of gold and flutter, and you couldn't predict when or where. Each time she descended, you'd leap into action, run and pounce, run and pounce, your tiny forepaws landing on yet another patch of butterfly-less clover. She eluded you, masterfully, but you didn't seem to mind.

As I watched you, something fluttered at the edges of consciousness, something from my own childhood—about the world in its color and motion, its magic. If a memory, it eluded like the butterfly. I couldn't capture it; I could only sense it.

And yet, you made it tangible. Even now, if I want to conjure it, I simply close my eyes, and remember *you*: besotted by a yellow butterfly, flitting after it across a meadow, leaping through the air, alighting in purple clover.

***

Your Joy Meditation

by Gerard Sarnat

Now nearly 80 years
later, every morning
when I close my eyes
and sit quietly for 20
minutes 'til timer goes
off; I do enjoy faces of
loved ones which bob
up as brightly lit circles
in front of me one-by-one
particularly six grandsons.

Fairytale Dreams

by Rena Weafer

"I found a fairy," my sister called from the backyard where she stood. We spent the day outside gathering supplies for fairy houses, an escape from the conflict inside our home. Sticks, moss and shells turned into a miniature house with the diligent work of our small hands. Acorn tops placed with intention for the fairies' headwear. Seashells filled with water for drinking and bathing. I cared for the fairies like I cared for my dolls, with the maternal instincts of a parentified eldest daughter in a war-torn family. Our childhood fantasies projected on the small structure, carrying our daydreams to those of mystic heights. My sister claimed she saw two fairies heading toward the hut as we parted. "But they're gone!" she said with a giggle. I retreated from our communal project as I heard her fable. She loved invention, but I preferred the truth.

My short legs strutted across the yard to my temporary sanctuary, the white sheet I laid on the ground with books stacked in piles of three or four. I liked to display my collected books for myself to peruse, as if I had a small library collection. I meandered through the books, thumbing for one that seemed of interest. My eyes glanced up from my white sheet, eyeing the line of trees marking the end of our property. My focus locked on the possibility of what the forest holds. The books I read, of magic and fairies, led to the outlook of wonder. My mind swirled with possibilities. Perhaps it held magic like the books in front of me. My solitude and contemplation provided space to process my repressed emotions through my imagination. My spirit bounced from one emotion to the next underneath my conscious processing. I stood to leap and twirl with the excess energy. The grass, soft in this area, tickled my feet as I pranced across the lawn. The trauma my child-self experienced resounded beneath the surface of my consciousness. My physical expression released this energy into something natural. I tip-toed across the grass and returned to my blanket where my books awaited me. Each one held a possible world to lose myself in, a new reality to help me escape. I selected one and propped it open, finding the first page.

*

I hold my dog-eared copy of *The Picture of Dorian Gray*, spine cracked with wear. Pen scrawls across each page, short black lines under quotes and quick memos in the margins. I place my bookmark with its soft white edges in my spot and shut the novel. I lie atop my sage, plush comforter and stare at the fan circling above me. My eyes follow each blade swinging before me, as my mind races from the previous day's events. The room's silence announces my private thoughts, as I imagine the words I didn't say and the opportunities I flat out refused. The nervous energy reverberates around my head, craving release. I jolt up from my trance and play a song from a playlist I made earlier. My limbs sway to the music before my feet dance to the melody. They hop, skip and skid across the floor, an exaltation of pure nerves. I find rhythm in the beat of the music. The notes loosen the swirled knots in my stomach and head. A smile spreads across my face as I sing the lyrics. Yesterday's missed chances slip to the back of my mind, where I will return to them another time.

"Last night, damn, you were in my sex dreams," Lady Gaga sings from my speaker, sitting atop my kitchen table. I'm home alone for the first time this week, and I've never felt more free. My hips sway to her rhythm, as my hands grab my head, my long blonde hair. The freedom fuels my twirls around the kitchen, as I wait for my dinner to finish cooking on the stove. The taste of solitude lingers on my tongue. Its sweet reminiscences of freedom were a luxury unknown to me as a child. My childhood fantasies of solitude and autonomy finally realized, like it wasn't outlandish after all. With the sudden realization, my energy radiates into movement, a natural consequence.

***

"Joy is fever, is tremor, is her lover's soft mouth pressed hard against hers,"

~ Betty Stanton

Fiestas en la Cocina (Parties in the Kitchen)

by Christin Marie

We dance and play like laughter ringing
Take my hand, turn up the volume.
Resume...
 your neck on display,
red meat, out for me to eat,
rare, with succulent flavor
I make you my dinner.

Feast–
 'cause that's what we do best–
freedom to indulge
with sensory-tuned tastebuds
 and timbres flying...
A meal without clothes is today's speciality.

Twirl me, move me
bend my hips to follow your rhythm
I grab hold of your thighs and create a stir–
 the melody of my concoctions.
Original, inspired
resourceful at play,
a delicate flavor to explode in your mouth.

Another sip, another gulp
 thread me through then let me unwind
see me spin in socks, I'm spun
then serve me up
 and garnish with kisses.

The oven's warm,
 and so are we
alight in music, smells, spells, symphony
Sparks fly from corner heights–
 simmer with me just a while longer...
for I've been cooked through,
juices still lingering.
Come slurp me up
 for no one should live without the food of love.

Let Me Tell You What I Love

by Annmarie Kelly

after Fanny Howe

That moment when I first lie down in bed and the hardships of the day and that crick in my neck and ache in my back and all worries finally melt away.

Ice cream. All of it. Coffee and dark chocolate and mint and fresh strawberry and also cherry-chip, if we're feeling fancy, and the lemon sorbetto we ate on that hillside overlooking the Mediterranean when Katie and I hiked Cinque Terre, and it was so sour sweet I thought tartness might park on my tongue and lemon-tinge everything forever and I wouldn't have minded.

Foreign films. And live theater, not just Broadway or the West End but community theater, too, and anytime someone lifts their voice earnestly in song. Bonus points if they close their eyes. And old movies with dapper-hatted fellas like Spencer Tracy or Cary Grant, and notorious heroines who may or may not have been trouble from the start: Katharine Hepburn, Ingrid Bergman, Lauren Bacall. But also newer old movies, like *Four Weddings and a Funeral*, where Hugh Grant blinks so much, or *Moonstruck*, where Cher is dressed to the nines and Nicolas Cage yells about his hand. And old-school songs my mom wouldn't let me listen to: "Papa Don't Preach," or "Push It," or "Laid," by James. But also church hymns. Play "Here I Am, Lord" loud enough and I'll cry every time. And "Be Not Afraid"? Forget it. I'm broken before the chorus.

Floating weightless in an ocean or pool. And reading beneath an umbrella beside the sea. And weightlifting. I can't forget weightlifting. I started when I turned forty, after all three of my kids were born, and I learned that when I dip into a deadlift or jerk a power clean, I can't possibly think about

"Shared grief. I don't mean the pain itself, but the way my heartache and yours can find each other in the dark, even if we're strangers."

anything else. I can't hold a cell phone or wonder what's for dinner. I can only heave into that moment. Plus, I spent most of my life wishing myself smaller, wishing my waist smaller, and my boobs smaller, but when it comes to lifting, strong is the new skinny, and it's permission to take up space.

And popcorn, oh the popcorn. I get it without butter these days which is worse for my mouth but better for my heart. That large bucket at the theater is a single serving just for me. And afternoons spent nursing one strong cup of decaf coffee, which seems an oxymoron, I know, alongside any chocolate dessert.

Shared grief. I don't mean the pain itself, but the way my heartache and yours can find each other in the dark, even if we're strangers. It's like that beacon of sadness in you can find the brokenness in me, and we orbit there for a moment honoring each other's pain and knowing deep down it's only there because we were so greatly loved.

Big hair and leg warmers and shiny purple eye-shadow. I'm a child of the 80s after all. Reading myself to sleep. Blowing soap suds bubbles with children. Chewing gum. Snow outside when I'm

outside. Rain outside when I'm inside. Fireplaces. Not just their initial crackle, but that dull, warm burn. A newly sharpened pencil. A walk with a friend. The burden that lifts when term papers are all graded, and the semester finally ends.

And travel. I love to scamper. Flying to foreign cultures or far-flung beaches. I like the way my head feels when I voyage, the way my senses open to new tastes, smells, and vistas. I also love that I'm a little afraid when I travel, like it would be so much easier to curl up beneath a blanket instead of packing my suitcase. My couch is more comfortable than an airplane. But I love that I adventure anyway. And I adore road trips, too. The gas station snacks, the mile-marker monotony and drive-thru dinners. I love the kinds of deep conversations we have when we aren't looking directly at each other. And I also like road-tripping alone. I'll sing every show tune or rock anthem with windows wide open on any ribbon of highway. I'm my own good company.

I love laughing with people who know me from before, like my one friend who calls me her 'trusty dire wolf' after a bizarre wine tasting years ago, and my other friend who'll tease me forever about my esoteric Shakespeare answer ("Cymbeline") when I interviewed for a teaching job at a high school in Seattle. And I love that feeling around a dinner table when all the food's been eaten, dessert has come and gone, and everyone stays. I love when people linger somewhere long after they could have left, because we're so full of the utter joy of being together in that extra, stolen time. No one dashes to pay the sitter or ducks off to bed for an early meeting. We don't get nearly as many nights of overtime friendship as you'd think.

There are words I love. Like Smurfy and Possibility and Storm and Hope. And song titles, like "Hakuna Matata" and "The Devil Went Down to Georgia" and "Wishing You Were Somehow Here Again." I like the feel of words in my mouth. And names, so many names, like Calliope and Fletcher and Rutherford and Reginald and Francesca and Santiago and Scheherazade. Imagine anyone lingering for 1001 nights over your stories.

Talking to strangers.

***

At My Grandma's I Used to Make the Orange Juice

by Ashley O'Neal

A concentrate. The frozen kind
that seals with a little plastic

band along the rim. I pull the
plastic ring and wedge my

fingernails between the lid
and cardboard tube, pour

the contents into the pitcher,
measure water to dilute things

properly.

I imagine the delicate glasses
everyone will sip from between

bites of toast. While I stir I bring
the silver lid to my lips and

feel the heavy flavor race up
my tongue. I lick it clean. Syrup

clings to my lips and they
shine. The best is mine.

"I crave a simple life, little fuss,
no clutter, few dire needs,
priorities set to whatever brings
laughter and awe."

~ Carolyn Chilton Casas

Six AM at the YMCA Pool

by Darin Murphy

Since my separation from Brian, I've gotten into the habit of going to the YMCA first thing in the morning. There are a handful of old men lined up at the door that early. Each of them long retired and habituated to predawn workouts because they can't sleep. My son, Zeke, is up half the night playing Fortnite and sleeps late, so he doesn't miss me. I come already in my swimsuit under my clothes and go right to the pool deck, strip down, and use the ladder to climb in. I'm still too tired to dive with that big, violent splash of bubbles. The easing in, transitioning from the heaviness of sleep to lightness and buoyancy, is what I like best. I take three waist flotation belts that small children use when learning to swim and tie them around my hips so they cover my stomach. I take two blue foam dumbbells and hold one in each hand, and lean onto my back so the water, belts, and the dumbbells hold me in a float. This is how I stay. Floating. No slow walking like the old lady aerobics that starts at eight AM, and no heavy armed laps like the old men who I hear begin their own descent into the water and slowly, so slowly, swim lap after lap. The old men always swim the crawl stroke that leaves them looking like bobbers drifting down the lanes. I shut my eyes and let those pool noises drown everything out. From time to time, I drift into the lane divider and kick away, but I want to move as little as possible.

Breathe.

Breathe.

Breathe.

Nothing else.

No paying attention to the world, or the past, or the day ahead.

Breathe and try to quell the quickening panic of having to reset my entire life.

Before the old men got used to me, they would tap me on the head or shoulder when I was in their path. Now they wait for me to drift by, swim around, or, if feeling playful, dive and try to swim underneath me like bespeckled manatees. They smile and nod to me in the morning, but I suspect they tell jokes about me in the locker room, as my motionlessness is odd to them.

I do this for up to an hour. Until my body chills. My fingers and the bottoms of my toes prune. Then I work my way to the ladder and begin to pull myself up, my body now heavy. The act feels willful, like I am fighting to start the day, not rolling confused and unready into it. Then the rest of the day, whenever I am stressed, or distracted, or feel that spiraling shift toward sadness rear up, I lick my finger and rub my skin to find the smell of the pool waiting there for me.

***

Spoonstruck
by Ellen Notbohm

Perhaps I was a magpie in a previous life; I'm drawn to the shiny bits. However small, however far afield from my range of vision, on any random ramble through parks, pioneer cemeteries, pebbled shorelines, and pathways, I find them. Most often, they disappoint. A corner torn from yet another foil bag of chips. A fallen screw or wingnut. A bottle cap, a pop tab.

But today, I must ask: Did you lose a spoon? A shiny, stainless steel spoon? In a parking lot, near the playground and the baseball field, quite a way from the picnic area. Your spoon almost made it back to your car, and then ...

Don't pick it up, my husband says. *It's dirty. And the owner might come back for it.*

But you weren't coming back for it, were you? From the light stippling of damp dirt, I can see it's been there a while. No cat, no fiddle. No cow, no moon. The dish ran away, solo. Did you forget its existence entirely? Or did you miss it but deem it not worth the effort of scouring a 16-acre park?

I deferred to my husband in the moment, but once home, I abruptly "remembered" some urgent errands. And there was your big ol' spoon, waiting for my return.

What was this upsized utensil's last gig? Dishing out potato salad? Jello? Baked beans? Not a greasy spoon, this one. It glints at me through the grime. Perhaps it got a rinse after completing its task. Or maybe it sat the picnic out, unused. Ignored. Unneeded.

Did it tumble from your basket unnoticed? Or did it stealth-slide over the side and stay behind because I needed to find it?

See, I'm at a difficult time in my life. I need to believe something's at work that's bigger than what's directly in front of my face. I know what a fork in the road means. But what does a spoon in a parking lot mean?

Plenty, it seems. A little research reveals that many cultures recognize the bowl and handle of the spoon as symbolizing feminine and masculine principles, respectively. When taken together, they personify the harmony of the universe.

I delve further. Spoons and their myriad uses and meanings, both practical and metaphysical, are present in every culture in the world. The spoon is an implement of nourishment and sustenance, suggesting a time of abundance, in some form, may be at hand. The handle also symbolizes support, a sign that one is not alone, that there are helpers all around.

Now that's some dollop of whipped creed. Do I embrace this new-found wisdom? Or do I cave to the know-it-all snark of artificial intelligence, whose search engine summary decrees:

> *Finding a spoon refers to simply locating a spoon that was previously misplaced or lost. It doesn't carry any specific cultural meaning or superstition beyond the practical act of recovering an object.*

And yet, below this smug certitude, in tiny print—the caveat:

> *AI responses may include mistakes.*

Stick a spoon in it; it's done! I laugh, pivoting toward harmony, abundance, and discovery.

***

A Conversation with Olivia Ho

interviewed by Kirsty Anne Richards

Olivia Ho is a PhD candidate in English Language and Literature at University College London. Her research focuses on the interstitial city in urban speculative fiction. She was formerly arts editor and chief book reviewer at *The Straits Times* newspaper in Singapore. She has been published in *Textual Practice, Wasafiri, Literary Review*, and more. She posts about books on Instagram as @ohomatopoeia.

Kirsty Anne Richards: Your PhD research focuses on "interstitial spaces" in urban fiction. This feels deeply connected to our theme, where the "in-between" moments are often where we find pockets of joy and personal reflection. Can you share how you find the poetry and possibility in these literary gaps?

Olivia Ho: I'd like first to clarify what I mean by 'interstitial space'. I derive my definition of 'interstitial' from the Latin *intersistere, inter* meaning 'between' and *sistere* 'to stand'; it is an in-between space, but it is not merely in between. For me, an interstitial space is a space, usually a small or minoritarian one, that intervenes between bigger, more established, more powerful spaces. These spaces are not necessarily joyful or magical, and I don't wish to romanticise them as such. In fact, they are often difficult and precarious spaces to be in, and there are many who have no choice but to exist in them. What interests me is this notion of intervention – how these spaces might be transformed from being passive, residual waste spaces to actively intervening in how we live in the city (and again, this might be positive, negative, or both at the same time). One way this happens is through making these spaces visible, and that is where the poetry and possibility of gaps come into play.

K: Thank you for clarifying. Italo Calvino's book, *Invisible Cities*, which you are examining for your PhD, is built on the idea that play and imagination reveal the hidden, emotional layers of a place. Moving from the page to the pavement, so to speak, how has this concept shaped your own perspective, and what is one practice you'd recommend for us to see the 'invisible cities' of memory and meaning in our own everyday lives?

O: It's not particularly groundbreaking, but I like to walk in cities, randomly and without purpose. You might call this flanêrie or psychogeography or what have you. I like to do this while practising what Anna Tsing calls 'arts of noticing' (she says this in reference to looking for mushrooms, but it applies more broadly to attending to the ways in which we are entangled with our life-worlds). There are so many hidden aspects to cities that you will notice if you pay attention, and that is why I find cities constantly wonderful.

Calvino's writing has a ludic, combinatorial quality that has led his work to be characterised as postmodern and 'playful'. At the same time, I don't believe he is entirely without political weight. I think Calvino was deeply concerned with problems of urbanisation, such as overpopulation or homogenisation or the degradation of the environment. Yet *Invisible Cities* handles these heavy issues with such lightness. We live in late-stage capitalism, witness to multiple unfolding genocides. I dream of learning to live in lightness, but without losing sight of the ground.

K: That's incredibly powerful. I think it is also important to remind ourselves of the lightness in life, even when exposed to the horrors. It makes fighting against the negativity more worthwhile as we have something positive to move toward and to keep us grounded. Thinking about your research, can you tell us about a real-life "interstitial space" that you've personally found joy, peace, or inspiration in? What was it about that specific, perhaps overlooked, place that made it feel so special?

O: At UCL, when I was an undergraduate, there used to be a space called the Garage Theatre Workshop, which was a student-run black box theatre. It was very small, wedged in between the buildings of the Bartlett, with a seating capacity of maybe 60 to 70 people. It was built and run entirely by the students of UCLU Stage Crew – we would do maybe eight to ten productions a term, with a different society putting on a different show every week, after which we would paint the floor and change the seating and start over again. Tickets cost three pounds. Generations of student theatre-makers learnt the ropes in the Garage. It was a space in which you could experiment, and which you also had to learn to do everything yourself, because nobody would do it for you. I learnt how to design a lighting rig and drill wood, and operate a jigsaw there. Because we had keys to the space, we basically lived in there. I wrote my essays in the tech box; I studied my notes on the tops of ladders. In the winter, we would rig starlettes to keep us warm.

The Garage Theatre Workshop was destroyed in 2014, after I left UCL, to make way for an expansion of the Bartlett. Interstitial spaces are often transient like that. It doesn't mean they didn't exist to begin with, or that what happened in them didn't matter. It was our theatre, and it lives on only in our memories, like so many lost places do.

K: That's a beautiful reflection. It often saddens me when spaces which meant so much to us get torn down or repurposed into something different from what kept us going there. But then I think it also makes room for something new to birth itself and provide memories and experiences for a different community. It becomes both a feeling of grief and hope, and always a feeling of being honoured to be part of whatever it was in that moment. Your work seems like a form of archaeology, uncovering the hidden stories and possibilities buried in the urban landscape. So tell me, does this practice of looking for hidden layers in cities change how you move through your own environment? Does it make the world feel more enchanted?

O: I do think of cities as palimpsestic, yes.

K: And these in-between spaces are often unregulated, unplanned, and free from commercial purposes. In that sense, is finding and claiming these spaces—both in literature and in life—a subtle act of liberation from the rigid, productive structures of modern society?

O: Yes, but again it is not a process I would entirely idealise. Interstitial spaces are also easily dominated and used for oppressive purposes.

K: That's a good point to remember. Going back to your work, you've moved from the fast-paced world of daily journalism to the more contemplative realms of academia and librarianship. This seems like a deliberate shift in rhythm. What self-care practices became essential in making that transition, and what did you have to "unlearn" about productivity?

O: In journalism, there is very little room for work-life balance. You are on call practically 24/7 to respond to breaking news, and you simultaneously have to find the time for longer-form reporting. I found it to be fulfilling work, but I had no room in my life for anything else; I did not know who I was without the work. Leaving journalism for academia has involved learning to centre my own research and my own writing. I've also learnt to not treat suffering as a form of validation. You do not have to suffer to be worthy. That helps nobody, least of all you.

Image on the left:
Book: Katabasis by R. F. Kuang
Dress: "Grey Stuff" Ballgown
from Rougerooi

Image on the right:
Book: Victorian Psycho by Virginia Feito
Victorian cape from Rebecca Sweeting
at Frock Me! Vintage Fair

K: Yes, I agree exactly with your observation that we don't have to suffer to be worthy. This is something I still have to remind myself, too, that working harder or longer does not make me more valuable, and a rested self, at least for me, leads to more creativity and productivity. Tell me, are there particular causes, values, or messages that you feel compelled to highlight through your work?

O: I believe in multiplicity. I believe there are so many ways to be, and we have to do our best to let these multiple ways of being exist, whether that's in terms of other cultures or genders or bodies or so on. I believe we cannot be silent about genocide, whether that is in Palestine or Sudan or the Congo or too many other places. I believe we are all deeply entangled with other human and non-human lives. I believe we must try to live while doing the least amount of harm to others and to the one precious planet we live on. This is, of course, very difficult. Still, we must try. Calvino, at the end of *Invisible Cities*, describes the 'inferno' created by so many of us living together, and adds that there are two strategies to deal with this: the first is to unsee the inferno; the second, which is risky and 'demands constant vigilance and apprehension', is to learn to see who and what is not inferno, and then 'make them endure, give them space'. Fundamentally, this has become my ethos: to make endure and to give space.

K: I love that! One thing I learnt while working on this business is that we can do anything and everything, and also that we can weave our values into our work; it doesn't have to be separate compartmentalisations of ourselves. Your work, for example, spans the deeply analytical (PhD), the organisational (librarian), and the creative (writing). This requires mental shifting. So, what is a non-negotiable daily or weekly practice that helps you return to yourself and find grounding amidst these different modes of thinking? Or do they all complement each other?

O: Every morning I go walking and I drink good coffee. If I don't do this, I can't write.

K: I think this also points to how much of our physical and psychological selves are intertwined. If one part is not getting its needs met, the other will suffer. I also want to talk about how your personal style is distinctly vintage. What joy do you find in curating your life and wardrobe from the past? Is it a form of storytelling for you?

O: In terms of vintage, I am especially drawn to styles from the 1920s to the 1960s, in part because these are all eras that produced some of my favourite works of art (for instance, I am a massive fan of film noir), in part because clothes produced in these periods were usually made to last. Vintage clothes often carry traces of their previous owners; for example, you can see from the inside where they have been repaired, or sometimes people stitch their names into collars. They are like texts of other people's lives, in a way.

K: Oh, I have never thought of it that way. At least not with clothes. But I do prefer older furniture as it too was built to last and holds so much history and memory in the making of the piece. You also match your vintage style to your current read, which feels like a very intentional, playful form of curation. Is this a way of physically wearing your intellectual and aesthetic world? Where does the inspiration for these specific pairings come from?

O: I think the intellectual world can often be rather snobbish about fashion, particularly when it's worn by a woman. I started my Instagram because I wanted people to respond to books the way they might to posts about outfits or make-up (I was, at the time, obsessed with videos in which people test lipstick shades), and I thought it would be fun to try and bridge the two. The pairing is always guided by the book cover; I try to build the image around that. I often think of the photograph Eve Arnold took of Marilyn Monroe reading *Ulysses;* a lot of people accused her of what we might now call 'performative reading', but I think it's entirely possible that she simply loved literature – she had a personal library of more than 400 books – and at the same time was keenly aware of how she was seen as one of the most beautiful women in the world, and the purposes to which that beauty might be turned.

K: Speaking of, in a world that often values the new and the now, choosing vintage can feel like a gentle rebellion. Does it feel that way to you?

O: I try not to buy new clothes. I find fast fashion horrific; it's a major source of environmental waste. Nearly everything I buy is secondhand or vintage; people also give me a lot of hand-me-downs when they're trying to declutter. My approach to fashion is one of serendipity; if it comes to me, I'll try to make it work. This extends to a lot of my life, which is guided by serendipity.

K: Ooh, I love that. As a book reviewer, you're constantly reading. How do you protect the pure, pleasurable joy of reading for yourself when it's also part of your work? What does your "guilty pleasure" read look like?

O: To be honest, it got pretty bad when I was working simultaneously as the chief book reviewer and assistant editor at *The Straits Times*. It was like a constant avalanche of new books, not all of which I wanted to read. I came quite close to burnout, which is an awful way to feel towards something you love. I am now in the happy place of getting to

Image on the left:
Book: Cahokia Jazz by Francis Spufford

choose what I want to review. Outside of academic research, I read about ten books a month, which is a pleasant pace for me, and review/post about maybe half of that. I don't have "guilty pleasure" reads any more, because all my reads are chosen for pleasure. That said, maybe I have a "guilty pleasure" in television? Recently, I've really enjoyed binge-watching *Slow Horses*.

K: I haven't seen that show, but I heard it's good (and is also adapted from a book!). Art is art, no matter the medium. So tell me then, what is a book, piece of music, or work of art that has profoundly shaped your perspective, and why did it resonate so deeply?

O: Artemisia Gentileschi's painting *Judith Slaying Holofernes*, which I've known about for a decade and got to see last year in person at the Uffizi in Florence. The sheer power of that painting, especially in person, cannot be overstated: the visceral muscularity of it, the unflinching violence of the act, the way the two women are working together to hold the man down. It's compounded by the knowledge of what Artemisia herself went through, as a rape survivor who subsequently endured a very public, brutal trial in order to get justice and reclaim her life – and at the same time, you can't reduce the meaning of the painting to her biography. It's a masterpiece by an artist at the absolute top of her game.

K: I know it is an impossible choice, but tell us about one of your favourite books, and why it has stuck with you?

O: My favourite book of all time is *The Lord of the Rings* by J. R. R. Tolkien. (The Peter Jackson adaptations are also my favourite films of all time.) I love the depth of world-building, how he invented multiple languages and mythologies and lore. (It led me to study Old English, because I wanted to see where Tolkien had got his inspiration.) At the same time, it is a simple, timeless story about courage and resistance in the darkest of times.

K: *The Lord of the Rings* is the best book(s) of all time, in my opinion. Truly spectacular to invent such a detailed world, languages, and his message is a classic tale of good vs. evil. A great choice! Finally, in the spirit of our issue: what is a hobby or practice you engage in for the sheer, unproductive delight of it? Something that is purely for *your* spark?

O: I love to go dancing! I have been doing belly-dance for 15 years now, and more recently I have taken up swing-dancing – both of these are social dances with deep cultural history in terms of their Arab and African-American roots, which I have really appreciated learning more about. I love dancing with other people, and seeing how our bodies respond to music and to one another. It's a different way of making space.

***

You can find Olivia here:
Instagram: @ohomatopoeia /
@goodenoughlibrary

Image above:
Book: Cinder House by Freya Marske

Our Time

by Tony Ruffo

Praise be that banged-up balcony,
Vaguely illuminated under the warm
Glow of lights wrapped around
Steel bars.

Inhale.
Snowballed smoke snakes into your soul.
Exhale.
Clouds envelop the chill of Fall.

We don't ever have to come down.
The wonderful whiff of flower,
The incessant sting when inhaling,
The hacking of horrid coughs.

Inhale.
Bring that burn into your bodies.
Exhale.
Let that skunky-scent swim free.

Praise be that banged-up balcony,
Engulfed in clouds of enjoyment.
The warm glow of burning paper,
The sweet touch of a sweetheart.

I Burned Your Card Today

by Tate Gebokoff

I've been lying to myself for nine years, mother. I tell myself
that you don't visit me in my dreams,
but that's not true. You are with me every night: my clenched jaw,
my restless sleep, the intrusions before sleep,
the waking doubt. Only now, I know you. I know you, now.
I wanted to reach out to you into whatever lightness
you've become. But you are not light. You never were. Only heavy pressure on my shoulders.
When I strip everything down, underneath all
that I've put on, what remains is anger at you. What you took and what you left.
And this morning, when you came to me, sharp
and full of doubt, I saw you for the first time. I took my 30th birthday card,
along with the card you gave me when I left home,
and the remembrance card that my father and my sister made without me.
And I burned them. I turned you to ash again.
To smoke. I released you. I release you. I burned them, burned you,
and I felt relief. A feeling of happiness. Happiness without you.
My clothes and hair smell like smoke, and that smoke is the freshest air I've ever breathed.
The smell of freedom. I gave you back to the wind,
so I may stand on my own solid ground,
and seize myself from my nine years of unrest. I am happy without you.
I am happy without you.
I am happy without you.

The Currency of Sweet Things

by Min Ko

My mom always handed me a coin. Just one. A 100-won coin, cool and round in my small palm.
With that coin, I bought milk caramels the most.

There were two types of milk caramels. One had Japanese characters with a yellow background, a small square-shaped box that opened like a drawer. Everything about this caramel was special, even the packaging. But they were 50-won more expensive. So, I couldn't buy them with the 100-won coin my mom gave me.

Instead, I bought the 100-won blue-packaged caramels. Those had only Korean characters. This one was shaped long, like a chewing gum package. When you opened it, there were seven rectangular pieces lined up, making the whole box elongated.

My happiest moment in life was when I opened a new caramel, and my saddest was when the last caramel disappeared in my mouth.

Sometimes, I bought round moon bread for 100-won. Moon bread consisted of two round-shaped soft bread pieces sandwiched together with white sweet cream inside. I was always disappointed and stressed about the small amount of cream. Then, peanut butter sandwiches came out.

They were incredibly soft with sweet peanut cream between white bread slices. I threw away the bread crust and ate the cream and the middle, feeling complete happiness.

For me, my mum was milk caramel, my mum was moon cake, and peanut butter sandwich. She was sweet, very sweet.

I realize now that those caramels were my first act of resistance. In a house where my father's rage could explode at any moment, where my mother disappeared into bottles hidden in closets before disappearing altogether, those seven pieces of candy became my universe. I would line them up on my palm, counting them like prayers. Seven chances at sweetness. Seven moments of control.

But here's the truth: I ate them fast. So fast. One after another, barely tasting, just needing. No one had taught me patience. No one had shown me how to wait. I'd chew through the first, then the second, then the third—my mouth working frantically, as if someone might take them away. As if the sweetness might disappear if I didn't consume it immediately.

I wanted them to last forever, but my body knew only urgency. This was the paradox of being seven and already starving for something I couldn't name. The caramels disappeared into me like everything good in my life—too quick, too desperate, leaving only the ghost of sweetness and the weight of wanting more.

"In the corner store, I held the power of choice. The blue package or moon bread. Seven caramels or one perfect peanut butter sandwich. This tiny economy of joy belonged only to me."

pleasure
/ˈplɛʒə/

<u>noun:</u> a feeling of happy satisfaction and enjoyment; enjoyment and entertainment, as opposed to necessity; an event or activity from which one derives enjoyment; sensual gratification.
<u>adjective:</u> used or intended for entertainment rather than business.
<u>verb:</u> give sexual enjoyment or satisfaction to.

My father would have called it greed, this desperate consumption. But it wasn't greed—it was survival. Each caramel eaten quickly was proof that I could have something, anything, before it was taken away. Before my mother disappeared again. Before the next explosion. Before the world reminded me that nothing good lasted.

That 100-won coin my mother pressed into my palm, I understand now what it meant. For her, it was perhaps the price of freedom. One hundred won to occupy her child for an hour, maybe two. Time to disappear into her own desperate needs, her own endless wandering through a life that had trapped her.

She was so young then, younger than I am now. A woman who'd never been allowed to discover who she was, married off and became a mother before she'd finished becoming herself. That coin was her ticket too, not to caramels, but to moments where she didn't have to be anyone's mother, anyone's wife. Just a woman walking Seoul's streets, searching for something she'd lost before she knew she had it.

For me, that same coin meant pure possibility. In the corner store, I held the power of choice. The blue package or moon bread. Seven caramels or one perfect peanut butter sandwich. This tiny economy of joy belonged only to me.

We were both buying time, my mother and I. She with her coin, me with my caramels. Both of us were desperate for sweetness in different forms. Both of us ate too fast, afraid it would disappear.

This is what they don't tell you about children in difficult homes: we become architects of joy, even messy, imperfect joy. We build it from rushed moments, from coins and candy wolfed down too quickly, from the sugar rush that proves we're alive. We create it not with patience or mindfulness, but with desperate hunger. And that hunger—that urgent need for sweetness—is its own form of resistance.

My mother gave me that coin and disappeared, sometimes for hours, sometimes forever. But in that gesture was an accidental gift: she taught me that joy could be bought for 100-won, even if you had to eat it fast. She taught me that sweetness existed, even if you couldn't make it last. She taught me that sometimes, the radical act isn't savoring, it's the grabbing, the claiming, the insistence on having something sweet even when the world offers only bitterness.

They say taste is the sense most connected to memory. But for me, memory tastes like urgency—like caramels eaten three at a time, like cream centers devoured before anyone could see, like the frantic sweetness of a childhood where nothing felt certain except the need for more.

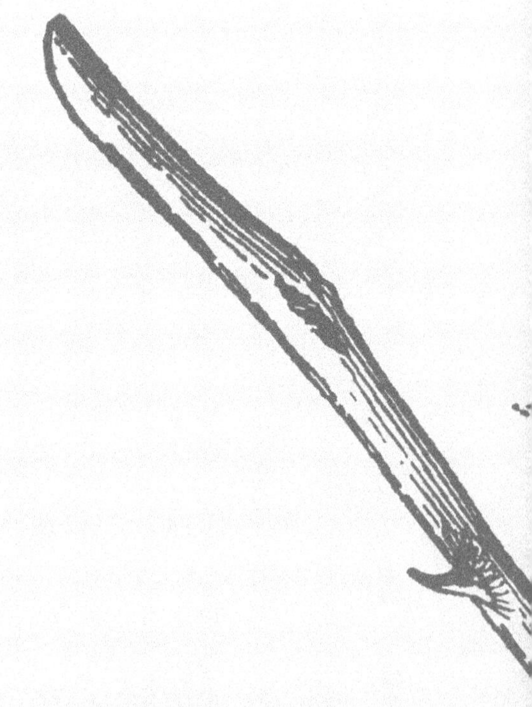

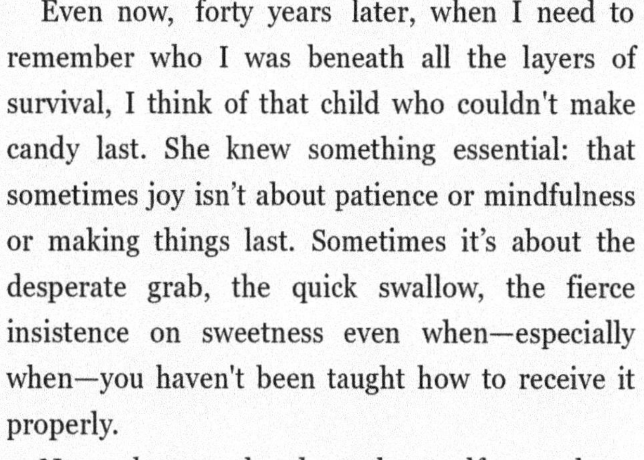

Even now, forty years later, when I need to remember who I was beneath all the layers of survival, I think of that child who couldn't make candy last. She knew something essential: that sometimes joy isn’t about patience or mindfulness or making things last. Sometimes it’s about the desperate grab, the quick swallow, the fierce insistence on sweetness even when—especially when—you haven't been taught how to receive it properly.

Now, when people ask me about self-care, about finding happiness in dark times, I think of those seven caramels in the blue package. How I turned them into my own rushed ceremony of need.
How even my impatience was a form of claiming what was mine.

That girl racing through her candy, counting empty wrappers like evidence of a life lived, she was already practicing radical joy. Not the Instagram kind, not the mindful kind, but the messy, desperate, real kind. The kind that knows sweetness is rare and grabs it with both hands. The kind that eats too fast because it knows how quickly everything disappears.

A girl, a coin, a choice at the corner store, and seven caramels that never lasted long enough. But they lasted. They existed. I held them, I chose them, I consumed them on my own terms, at my own desperate speed.

And that—that hungry, imperfect claiming of sweetness—was my first revolution.

***

My Sanctuary

by Aditi Y

"Crack", goes the joint,
As I break up bones and toss them behind;
I scream in perceived agony, as I pull out my fingernails one by one.
And then I tie my tendons to form a rope;
As strong as the sun.
My eyes, lips, nose and curls I leave to rot as if to prove they're beautiful; I hadn't extensively fought,
And with a sharp knife I scrape off my skin,
Its texture to that of rubber akin,
As now with my own body, a home I'll build.
My sanctuary,
From the sweat, blood, tears that came from within.

The High Untrespassed Sanctity of Space

by Fred Cheney

"Hold these two pieces of wood, boys, and tell me about them." We did as we were told and reported that the one with the reddish tint was heavier and seemed stronger. Mr. Batchelder took the pieces back and launched into his lesson. "So we have strong and heavy, or light and weak. But for an airplane, we need what?" Barely pausing, he answered his own question. "Well, we need light and strong, of course, and neither of these is quite right, are they?" We, members of Mr. Batchelder's class, obediently shook our heads from side to side.

Later, in another school lesson, we were exposed to the word *eccentric*, and our minds all formed an image of Mr. Batchelder. This year, he was building an airplane, and it was our favorite of all his projects. As usual, he involved us. He laid out the plans he'd gotten through *Popular Science Magazine* and explained them in detail. We sanded struts and helped stretch muslin over the frame, and helped paint the fabric with white lead paint.

We didn't go to his barn every day in the early '50s, because spring was also for baseball, but if it rained, or if we didn't have quite enough players for two good teams, we ended up at Mr. Batchelder's. He would give each of us a project and explain how it fit into the big picture, which was flight. Slipping "the surly bonds of earth," he called it, quoting from a poem.

Mrs. Batchelder would come out at some point with milk and warm peanut butter cookies. "Mr. Batchelder, you can't make these poor fellows work for no pay," she'd say. They always called one another Mr. and Mrs., and, since we knew their names were Eugene and Martha, we wondered what names they used when they were alone.

Then she would roll her eyes, nod in the direction of the skeletal plane, and say something like, "I'm fortunate, Mr. Batchelder, that you have the dream of being the first man in town to fly your own airplane. It keeps you out of my hair."

"It's not mere flying, Mrs. Batchelder; it's more a matter of joining 'the tumbling mirth of sun-split clouds,'" he answered, quoting from that poem again. We didn't know which of them had the more accurate view of it all, but our hearts were clearly with Mr. Batchelder.

Spring inched into summer, and school let out, and the plane acquired an engine, cables attached to flaps and rudders, a Plexiglas windshield, and a date for its maiden flight. One afternoon, we arrived, wondering if there was anything left to do on the plane. Mr. Batchelder was there painting the name "Martha" on the fuselage. "That's it, boys, tomorrow's the day that this jewel and I 'top the windswept heights with easy grace where never lark nor even eagle flew.'" That poem again.

The next day, when we arrived, the barn doors were shut, and Mr. Batchelder was sitting on a wooden crate, staring down into the dirt. Nobody spoke, but our expressions asked the question on all our minds. "There won't be any flying today... or any other day, boys. Mrs. Batchelder says it's too dangerous. She's right, you know. I don't know anything about flying. She says it's an emergency waiting to happen."

We were stunned. Devastated. Paralyzed. And then Dennis Paul said, "So we won't see you 'chase the shouting wind along'?" Bobby Coe asked, "'No 'eager craft through footless halls of air'?" We had learned some engineering and some poetry, and we were the better for it.

Slowly, Mr. Batchelder rose, walked to the house, and disappeared inside. In somewhere between three minutes and three days, he re-emerged, a tentative smile on his lips. "I'm going to taxi the plane down there in the field, not fly it, mind you, just taxi down and back."

This was clearly the best we were going to get, and we were thrilled with just this much. We attacked the barn doors, pushed the plane out, and stood back as Mr. Batchelder spun the propeller. The engine caught immediately, as eager for this moment as the rest of us. He climbed up into the cockpit and strapped on a leather hat and goggles. He looked as much the pilot as Charles Lindbergh.

The engine revved, the plane shook, and began to move. Mr. Batchelder went to one side of the big field and began to taxi straight across in front of us. It bounced some, and the wings rocked side to side, looking for all the world like planes we saw in newsreels at the movie theater. At the end of the field, he locked the brake on one wheel, revved the engine more, and the plane turned around for another taxi.

About halfway across the field, two principles of physics coincided. The slight increase in the plane's velocity met with a sudden gust of headwind, and, wonder of wonders, the *Martha* did indeed "slip the surly bonds of earth." We cheered insanely, hugged one another, and a screen door slammed behind us. Mrs. Batchelder made her way across the yard.

Up in the air, Mr. Batchelder realized that he really had not prepared adequately for this turn of events, but remembering what he'd read during the installation, he increased the flaps and cut the engine speed. The plane came down hard, bounced back up, and came down again, this time nose first, breaking the propeller and tearing one wing loose. And that's how it stayed, propped up like an acrobat standing on its head.

We got to the plane a few steps ahead of Mrs. Batchelder and guided our hero's feet down onto the ground. Then we backed away as the distance between Mr. and Mrs. Batchelder reduced to nothing. "Are you hurt, Mr. Batchelder?"

"Not at all. Are you angry, Mrs. Batchelder?"

"I'll only be angry if that thing can be repaired. Now, come help me put together a tray of cookies for these boys." And with that, she put her arm around his waist, and the two of them walked across the field and up to the house.

The plane stayed there like that the rest of the summer, a stark contrast to its proud moment in "the high untrespassed sanctity of space."

***

High Flight

"Oh, I have slipped the surly bonds of earth,
And danced the skies on laughter-silvered wings;
Sunward I've climbed and joined the tumbling mirth
of sun-split clouds – and done a hundred things
you have not dreamed of – wheeled and soared and swung
high in the sunlit silence. Hovering there
I've chased the shouting wind along and flung
my eager craft through footless halls of air.

"Up, up the long delirious burning blue
I've topped the wind-swept heights with easy grace,
where never lark, or even eagle, flew;
and, while with silent, lifting mind I've trod
the high untrespassed sanctity of space,
put out my hand and touched the face of God."

By John Gillespie Magee, Jr.

Euphoria
by Betty Stanton

She rises as if called by another world, tilts upward, unsure if her body belongs to earth or to sky. Breath floods her chest, a force so sudden it feels like a fracture, but light clings to her ribs, trembling, each vein carrying a current that threatens to burst her open. They said joy was gentle, a candle in the dark, but she knows better. Joy is fever, is tremor, is her lover's soft mouth pressed hard against hers, both of them shivering with too much sweetness. There is rebellion and power in that kiss: a surge that splits her spine into rivers of fire, a burning refusal to kneel. She rises again and again and again and again, the unbearable sweetness of being carried past silence, past shame, into the radiance of another body. Their bodies lift, shadows lagging behind, bones porous as honeycomb, hollow as a bird's. Gravity has no grip on them. They are rising above.

“We need Joy as we need air. We need Love as we need water. We need each other as we need the earth we share.”

~ Maya Angelou

Moxie

by Gabriella Brand

I was supposed to talk to a Mr. Freddy about a job.

I had dragged myself to the other side of town, far from the university to the offices of Laugh-A-Gram, a small storefront entertainment agency wedged between a falafel joint and an H&R Block. In the dusty front window, there was a clown mannequin, a fluffy pig costume, some spilled confetti, and a couple of rubber chickens. Inside, the air smelled of latex balloons.

A friend, hearing that I was looking for extra work, had encouraged me to apply. She assured me that no experience was necessary, but I found myself hesitating at the door. This was not my kind of place. I was a graduate student who spent hours ensconced in a Gothic library, my nose in various 18th-century tomes. At the same time, I worked part-time as an adjunct French professor at a third-rate local college. I was a serious, cultured person, the kind of human being who conjugated irregular Latin verbs to put herself to sleep.

I found Mr. Freddy at his desk, yelling into a telephone. Behind him, a jumble of wigs, props, fuzzy suits, and huge polyester animal heads hung from metal racks. When he put the phone down, he looked me over and shook his head.

I started to introduce myself, using my friend's name as a reference.

Freddy interrupted with a snarl.

"You a teacha' or a student?" he asked.

Maybe my face conveyed a sort of schoolmarmish scowl.

"Kind of both," I said.

Freddy leaned back in his swivel chair. He narrowed his eyes.

"So, you're used to public spitting, right?" Freddy asked.

"Spitting?" I asked, slightly bewildered.

I looked at Freddy's face. He was now grinning broadly. I realized that he was testing me.

"Of course, I'm used to public spitting," I boasted. "Once I spat in the eye of a student in the back row just by saying the word *Robespierre*."

"So let me guess. You can't juggle, you can't sing, and you can't pratfall," said Freddy.

We went on like this for a few minutes. Was this an interview? Or was Mr. Freddy just a little bit crazy? I couldn't tell. Now and then, Freddy would hand me a prop, an "exploding" mustard jar or a fly swatter as large as a tennis racket. If I thought too much, I'd come up with nothing. My cerebral side got in the way. But if I let myself go, I could tap into absurdity.

Occasionally, we were interrupted by a phone call or the comings and goings of a costumed Marcel Marceau or a Raggedy Andy. As I listened to Freddy's interactions with his employees, I got the impression that he thought of himself as a show business mogul, a Ziegfeld or a Barnum. It became clear, however, that Laugh-A-Gram's scope was largely limited to providing costumed characters for local birthday parties, company picnics, retirement homes, and business conventions. The *Commedia del Arte* it was not. In those days, balloon delivery was a big deal as well, with most offices and institutions open to welcoming a costumed stranger, with no security checks.

“ ...I realized that the job was providing me with a chance to re-discover the imp that was part of my childhood. Once upon a time, I had been silly, mischievous, playful. But that joy had been scrubbed out of me by the Ivory Tower...”

As Freddy and I chatted, I could feel him measuring me with his eyes, but not in a lurid way. At five-foot-two, I was small enough to portray a duck or Little Bo Beep. I was also limber enough to function as a mime or a dancing penguin.

“I go by my gut,” said Freddy at the end of our meeting, “I think you’ve got the necessary moxie.”

I wasn’t sure what moxie was, but we shook hands.

Freddy immediately started to find gigs for me. A singing telegram at a wedding, a walk-around dressed as an ostrich for an insurance convention.

“We could use a Wise Owl for a Bar Mitzvah. Can you do it? Saturday afternoon?” he’d ask.

I was almost always available. Newly divorced women often don’t have much of a social life. On the weekends, or sometimes between classes, I was more than happy to earn a hundred bucks for a few minutes’ “work”. Especially work that was joyful and light-hearted.

“Pick up the costume around noon. Be on the set by 1:00 PM,” Freddy would say.

When he spoke to me, Freddy always made it sound as if he were talking to some movie star of old, Lucille Ball or Betty White. As if I were headed off to Universal Studios instead of the local VFW hall.

“Right, boss,” I’d say.

“Gotta run. The bookings are coming in fast and furious. A lotta great shows in the works,” Freddy would say as he hung up the phone.

I didn’t mind Freddy’s pretense of greatness. If anything, his illusion that Laugh-A-Gram was Hollywood added to the charm of the job.

Working at Laugh-A-Gram became a kind of Get Out of Jail Card for me. An escape from reality. In those days, I felt burdened by my responsibilities as a single mother, the stresses of teaching and fulfilling grad school requirements, the aching loneliness of a newly divorced woman. I was bitter that my husband had left. My feelings of having failed at marriage clung to me like smoke. I’d get dressed quickly in the morning in zombie-like fashion, throwing on nondescript clothing and sensible shoes so I could run from my child’s soccer game to the Stop & Shop, from a meeting with my thesis advisor to a faculty workshop.

*

My regular job provided little in the way of fun. While I thought I would love teaching, I found those particular college students quite dull. Or maybe it was just me. In any case, the curriculum at that institution was outdated and set in stone. It was hard to muster enthusiasm for explaining Alexander Dumas and *La Dame Aux Camélias* to a bunch of twenty-year-olds who didn’t know a camellia from a beer keg.

But the longer I worked at Laugh-A-Gram, I realized that the job was providing me with a chance to re-discover the imp that was part of my childhood. Once upon a time, I had been silly, mischievous, playful. But that joy had been scrubbed out of me by the Ivory Tower, or maybe

A Story of Trauma, Truth, and Triumph

Kathleen Hoy Foley's acclaimed trilogy offers a beacon of understanding for anyone touched by the legacy of sexual abuse. These books are more than a story—they are a FREE resource for healing, education, and hope.

- ***Woman in Hiding*** champions truth as personal and social advocacy.
- ***Breaking Through Silence*** serves as a vital mentor, guiding readers out of isolation.
- ***Forget About Heaven*** beautifully weaves together the physical and spiritual dimensions of recovery.

Answer the Call to Understand.
Receive your free digital copies of this essential trilogy.
Download instantly at:
https://mediumsinart.weebly.com/free-pdf-books.html
Follow Kathleen's writing on Substack:
https://substack.com/@thedarksideofasunnystreet

Prefer a physical copy? Simply request a free paperback through the website contact form.

just by growing up and abutting adult life. Laugh-a-Gram was the ultimate in make-believe. I could forget my worries when I took on the persona of Mrs. Duck. And there really were no rules. Freddy expected me to write my own material or come up with my own set of gags, a challenge that was quite a bit more relaxing and liberating than writing a doctoral thesis.

If I felt like singing, I sang. Even though I sing off-key, no one ever complained. If I felt like blowing a CEO a kiss, I never hesitated. If I wanted to see if I could still do a cartwheel, nothing stopped me from trying it in the hallway of the Old Folks Home, causing the residents to squeal or gasp with pleasure.

The motto of Laugh-A-Gram was *Put A Smile On It*. These words were stamped on all Freddy's contracts, and he usually repeated the slogan while sending me off to a new gig.

I soon learned that if I managed to leave an audience with really big smiles, the tips would be really big as well. But my greatest pleasure didn't come from the money. It came from bringing something to ordinary people, many of whom were weary, bored, discouraged, or just moping along. Sometimes I'd park my car, change from my regular shoes to my polka-dotted clown shoes or my chicken feet (you can't drive in oversized shoes) and start sashaying over to an office building where a person working in a brokerage firm on the 15th floor was about to get a surprise. Along the way, on the street, people who were just plodding through their day would see me. It was impossible not to see me. A clown or animal costume stands out in a throng of business types wearing three-piece suits and polished Cole-Haan shoes. It was rare not to catch their faces changing. Sometimes a full-toothed smile, sometimes a smirk, sometimes a grin as if they didn't want to get caught enjoying a memory of childhood or a vision of the absurd.

Sometimes I'd interact in a parking lot just for the heck of it. I'd do a little mime thing, or hug a light stanchion, or simply greet pedestrians with an exaggerated bow. The public's reactions made me happy.

Occasionally, people would hand me money out of the blue, in appreciation. I'd be leaving a Bar Mitzvah party, and somebody's uncle would come running after me, thrusting twenty, thirty, fifty bucks into my white gloved or fuzzy hands."You made the rabbi laugh," they'd say, or "You were the icing on the cake."

That kind of payment felt different from any other money I've ever earned. My professional salary was always direct-deposited. I had no physical relationship with it. But those Laugh-A-Gram tips were warm and alive. They came out of someone's pocket, reeking of Chiclets or Altoids, orange peels or tobacco, engine oil or laundry detergent. I started to think of those tips as funny money, earned with a kind of joy in my heart.

I derived a lot of pleasure from my moonlighting job, even though some people thought this line of work was "beneath me."

"Surely you could find further work in your professional field," a relative suggested. "Have you tried looking in *The Chronicle of Higher Education*?"

But I needed Laugh-A-Gram at that point in my life. Plus, I was never bored. This kind of low-level performing required spontaneity and creativity. I appreciated the opportunity to live lightly; to cultivate laughs, not erudition.

One day, Freddy called with desperation in his voice.

"The bookings are coming fast and furious," he said. "Could you do me a favor and work a Firemen's Association party? Like tonight? I know it's last-minute. But it's just fifteen minutes of clowning. That's all."

"Sure," I said. "You mean just a regular clown? For families? Red nose, big wig. Do a few gags, a little stage business?"

"Yeah, yeah," said Freddy, in his usual frenetic manner. "They have a gap before the main act. You'll keep 'em happy."

"Okay," I said.

"Put a Smile On It," he said, as he hung up.

I pictured a hotel ballroom full of firefighters and their families, maybe a child-friendly singer with a guitar as the main attraction.

When I arrived at the venue, I saw swarms of muscled men tottering around in the lobby, as if they were on a swaying ocean liner, holding onto the walls for support. I didn't see any female firefighters.

A few minutes later, I walked onto the stage. The audience was slouching on folding chairs placed around tables decorated with a miniature fire truck, an American flag, and a tray of raw vegetables and a creamy dip. There wasn't a child in sight. The room smelled of booze and ranch dressing.

I had been planning some nonsense, pretending to put out a fire. I'd even brought along a tin bucket. Now I needed to switch gears quickly.

I strode back and forth across the small stage, swinging my bucket. My mind was racing. Surely, I could come up with a bit of adult fireman-oriented humor. Something about hoses, maybe.

"What the hell is this?" came a voice from one of the front tables.

I ignored the heckler and continued my patter.

"I thought we were getting a stripper," shouted another voice.

One man started to beat his palms against the tablecloth. Others joined in. The pounding caused a couple of the miniature fire engines to slide off tables. Drinks spilled. Someone started booing.

Suddenly, I felt something spongy hit me on the side of the head. The firemen were throwing the

cherry tomatoes. Little flecks of creamy dip splattered my wig.

"Where's our stripper? Where's our stripper?"

The firemen were in an uproar. I felt I had no choice but to abandon ship. Stumbling in my ridiculous shoes, I headed off stage. I ended up dropping the tin bucket and leaving it behind as I made my way out of the building. I felt humiliated, but I wasn't hurt. Most of all, I feared facing Freddy. I suspected he would upbraid me for failing to leave the audience laughing.

But he didn't. He admitted that he had misunderstood the nature of the event.

"I screwed up," he said.

He patted my back and assured me that he knew all about performing.

"Sometimes you bomb," he said. "So whadya do? You pick yourself up and start all over again. That's show business. That's life."

Eventually, I said goodbye to Freddy and pursued a full-time academic job.

But I discovered that performing for Laugh-A-Gram gave me the confidence to bring my natural, innate humor into all my work, into all my interactions. I stopped teaching college students and discovered that zany energy works well with Middle Schoolers. I never worried about making a fool of myself – I'd already faced a room full of drunk firemen, I could do anything. In time, I got appointed to several leadership positions at independent schools, largely because I never feared giving a speech and I could think on my feet, although, by then, I refrained from doing cartwheels. I could face an audience of trustees with self-assurance and a smile.

Joy is there for the taking. You don't need oversized shoes, just a little imagination and a dose of moxie.

***

First Fruits
by Ella B. Winters

I started buying myself flowers
this year. Sacred offerings
of small, prickly roses,
pale carnations drowning
in baby's breath, bright tulips
in Spring, white lilies
on sale. Today,
exhaling August,
I presented myself with a constellation
of aster daisies. A bushy
bundle of pastel suns
overflowing
from the old Oktoberfest
stein that I use as a vase.
Golden centres clinging
to Summer, long limbs flailing
in all directions, grassy
and wild, drunk
on fresh water and a breeze
floating in through the still
open window. A bounty
to usher the Michaelmas, to worship
myself into a new cycle.

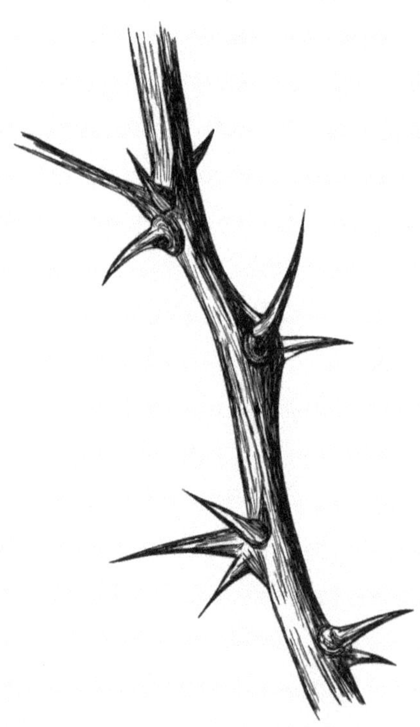

Winter Bath

by Carol Shannon

We put the winter blankets on the bed
And give ourselves morning fires with our coffee

But it's the afternoon baths that I need the most
Where I lie and soak and breathe
In between gratefulness and anticipation

Floating between the warmth and the cold
My body preparing for what I'm unable to see

Color Anomaly

by Oleg Olizev

Irkutsk City, Siberia. Summer 1986. I had just graduated high school when a new world opened to my desires and dreams. But not all at once. A little at a time, bit by bit.

Back then I thought life would unfold in a straight line: one exam, one school, one future. But the world has a way of testing how badly you want to belong. It doesn't always crush you. Sometimes it reroutes you toward places you never imagined, but that were quietly waiting for you all along.

Do you know that feeling, when the world takes its time to taste you?

No? Maybe you do. Loves me, loves me not. Lets me in, shuts me out.

Have you ever laughed at yourself for stumbling into a new world? For opening a door, only to hear it creak so loudly you wanted to step back?

I stumbled.

After finishing school, I enrolled in the Department of Biology at Irkutsk State University. But that wasn't the plan. This story began differently. I applied to medical school, but something went wrong.

Medical school. Fourteen applicants for every spot. Applicants had to pass six exams: four oral – Physics, the science of how the world moves; Chemistry, the science of how elements combine and break apart; General Biology, the science of how life is structured and functions; and a Foreign Language, the science of understanding the unfamiliar and making it your own. And two written: Mathematics, strict, like the steady rhythm of a metronome; and Literature, wild, like a river that refuses to be forced into pipes.

I believed I could pass. I stepped forward and I stumbled. An unexpected obstacle appeared. Murphy's Law. If something can go wrong, it will. A new requirement: a medical examination focused on smell and vision. I had never heard of these tests before and assumed they would be something like the routine military draft exam.

The examination room. I arrived early, one of the first. The written instructions I received said I had to be completely undressed. Why did they need me nude for a smell or vision test? When I asked where I should undress, they told me it wasn't necessary. Strangely, I felt relief. It was like stepping into a cage full of predators and realizing, for now, they weren't hungry. But the pause before humiliation didn't last long.

I was in the first room for less than a minute. They made me sniff formalin. Formalin, the stuff that traps flesh in eternity. I took a breath. The smell punched me in the nose, sharp and aggressive.

"What does it smell like?" The guy in the white coat watched me.

I froze. Smell like? How the hell was I supposed to know? How was a high school kid who had never handled a dead body, never opened a jar of preserved organs or tissue, supposed to recognize that scent? I had no clue. But instead of admitting it, instead of just saying, "I don't know this smell," I blurted out the first thing that popped into my head.

"Rose oil?"

Wait.

What the hell did I just say? But the words had already left my mouth, already turned into a fact I couldn't undo. A perfume bottle, the one my father brought back from Libya, that's what came to mind. Rose oil.

The examiner's reaction was immediate.

"What?" He leaned in, eyes narrowing.

I felt the shift, something sharp and dangerous, but it was too late to take it back.

"Rose oil..." I repeated, trying to shrug it off, to make it sound unimportant, less absolute. But the words just hung there, heavy as a dropped weight.

"Are you stupid, or just defective?"

Click. The mockery machine powered on. The nurse giggled. She threw him a look, as if waiting for more. I hesitated. I'd been caught off guard, like a defective part about to be tossed for failing quality control. How was I supposed to know? When do high school kids ever come across formalin? In chemistry class? No. In biology class? No. In morgues we were never taken to?

They had backed me into a corner, and I hadn't even realized when it happened. There was no way out. All I could do was stand there, watching the scene unfold, the screws tightening, the gears clicking into place, the whole machine grinding into motion, feeding off their laughter.

I just stood there, unsure. Had I already lost, or not yet?

"We're done here."

A snap. The sound of something locking into place.

"What the hell are you staring at? Get out. Next room. Next!"

The voice was harsh and metallic, like the slam of a garbage chute. I didn't get a chance to say anything. I didn't even get to ask what had just happened, why it had happened, what the point of it was. They just shoved me forward, onto the next section of the conveyor belt.

The Second Room.

An older woman. Impeccably neat. Gray eyes. She sat me down at a desk and opened a book filled with colorful circles. Rabkin's tables, a color vision test. A screening for color blindness.

First page, no problem. Second, fine. But then... The colors. The geometric shapes refused to form meaning. Like a secret code everyone else could read except me.

"You're color-anomalous."

Flat. Like a stamp on a rejection slip.

"What does that mean?"

"You have a deficiency in perceiving shades of green and red."

I blinked.

Like I had misread a traffic light and suddenly found myself under a car.

"You're defective."

Click. Judgment passed.

"You won't be accepted into any college or university."

"What?"

I couldn't believe it.

"Are you saying I need to see every color perfectly just to be a student?"

"I told you, it's a new regulation. Or do you have hearing problems too? Are you deaf?"

That was it: a rule and a wall that hadn't been there a second ago.

"Everything around me felt unreal, like a dream where someone guides you to a place you never thought of going, and somehow it turns out to be exactly where you need to be."

"You should go to a vocational school. They might take you there."

"Vocational school?!"

"Oh, and by the way, you're not allowed to drive either."

"What?!"

"Are you deaf? People like you aren't allowed to drive."

As if it wasn't enough to cut off my future, they had to make sure I stayed down.

"Move along! Next!"

Click.

I walked out and sat on the edge of a flower bed, my head buzzing, something in my chest tightening, my hands trembling as the tears burst out on their own like a broken pipe. I clutched my head in my hands, as if that could keep my thoughts from crumbling into dust.

Two girls walked past. They noticed me. They knelt down beside me.

"What happened?"

I exhaled, trying to explain between sobs:

"I'm color-anomalous—

Red and green—

They won't accept me into any college—

or university-y-y!"

"That's not true." Their voices were firm and steady, like a lifeline thrown into raging water.

"You can get into any college or university, just not medical school. If that's what you wanted, you might like the biology department at Irkutsk State University. Come on, we'll show you where it is."

I blinked.

"What's the competition like?" I asked.

"Lower than here, seven applicants per spot. Five exams, same as med school, but without physics."

My chances of becoming a university student had just shot up. The girls led me down Lenin Street, a wide and open street. I barely heard their voices. Everything around me felt unreal, like a dream where someone guides you to a place you never thought of going, and somehow it turns out to be exactly where you need to be.

And then they pointed. I looked up at an old and majestic building, a fusion of empire style, baroque, and Soviet constructivism. It looked as if different eras had agreed to live under one roof. Some parts were hidden behind thick, leafy trees, which made it look even more mysterious.

I forgot about my rescuers in an instant. A jolt sent me across the road, as if I were being pulled by a magnet.

The door. I pushed it open and stepped inside.

The building's interior was vast, dim, and cool, like an old cathedral where silence lives. The air carried the scent of aged wood and fresh paint, as if the past and present had merged in a single breath.

At the center stood a grand marble staircase, wide and luxurious. The banister was heavy, smooth, and cold. On the walls, paintings from the past century. The shores of Lake Baikal.

Silence.

I stood still. I felt the space and the weight of that silence.

In the distance, a door creaked open. The sound sliced through the air. Then came footsteps, sharp and steady, like the ticking of a metronome in an empty concert hall.

And then a middle-aged woman appeared, probably a faculty member.

I didn't let her say a word.

"Do you accept colorblind students?" I blurted it out, as if her answer would determine whether I existed or not.

She smiled. Like the first warm ray of spring slipping through a window.

"We accept everyone."

She smiled again. Like a breeze cutting through the stale heat of August. It was sudden, quiet, and almost impossible to believe.

That was the moment the ground stopped shifting. A door I never expected opened, and I walked through it. What I thought was an ending was only a turn in the path, a small one, but enough to lead me where I needed to go.

*

Ironically, a decade later, I would get my first real job in the United States by identifying color. At Yale University, my main task was staining and interpreting histological slides, tissue samples from both animals and humans. Not only did I master it, but my work was consistently among the most precise.

"These are the best histological preparations I've seen in twenty-five years," said a world-renowned professor.

Not a compliment, but a quiet undoing of everything they once told me I could not be.

After that, researchers began seeking out my eye.

What had once been called a defect had become my way of seeing. My way of belonging.

***

"We don't ever have to come down.
The wonderful whiff of flower,
The incessant sting when inhaling,
The hacking of horrid coughs."

~ Tony Ruffo

Angels

by Rita McDermott

What My Momma Told Me About Angels
Did your momma ever tell you
magnificent tales
about angels
that captured your imagination
when you were a child?
My momma once told me
as we watched the snowflakes fall
from the sky
that the angels were having a pillow fight
up in heaven.
I remember the time when we heard the thunderclap
during a storm
and cringed at the sight
of the brilliant bolt of lightning
when my momma told me the angels were bowling
up in heaven
"One of them got a strike!"
Momma also told me
one particular gray, cloudy day
as it started to rain
angels were crying in heaven.
On a gusty fall day
as we held on to our hats
and the leaves twirled on the ground
my momma told me
the angels were blowing the dust around
up in heaven.
To this day
during all our weather events
I still think of momma's tales
and think
How busy all those angels are
up in heaven.

Fernfully
by Robert Vivian

The arms of my reading glasses clicking together so softly like the kiss of a cue ball off the nine into the side pocket in the bliss of a perfect contemplative sound, the sudden drop away and disorienting feeling upon suddenly finding myself without a pen or paper in a moment of lyrical frenzy, even as the poetical vapors are rising and drifting away in front of me, before I can get their soul-tracks down on the page in the worst hand-writing in the history of this clamoring world, the simple word **and** because it connects all I love in a serial list that goes on forever, and, and, and another and another, and Kandinsky's line "He knew how to create a living being out of a teacup," and may I sip from such a cup until my dying breath and maybe even after in a crude, naked grave thriving with daisies and butterflies coming out of the cratered sternum of my chest, and the piping hot samovar of I, who am able only to offer this pent up sigh of gratitude streamside from a little creek in Northern Michigan so tiny and intimate, I tuck it inside my left elbow for safekeeping or rather hugged earthen awe; early mornings up north in early June and the lilacs blooming with delirious redolence drawing butterflies from every corner of the earth, may they hover around my heart forever as forever is accomplished in the chatter of chipmunks, so excited at being alive they pogo around the garden in endless play, and how this wild utterance keeps breaking and breaking apart to make more room for the surprising and unexpected, Rumi's guesthouse open to all comers, butterflies again and a perfectly rotund bumble bee bumping against the screen humpty-dumpty style, how the shadows of the Norwegian spruces tremble against the walls in pencil sketching's of dark and light shimmering all summer long and how I tremble with them back to first aching childhood, maybe these few pages I am given without my full awareness to ooze into making,

because were I more conscious of what I was doing I would screw it up, not even just me but somehow a mysterious we together, for one never writes alone or for oneself but always in hushed concert with some other heart or spirit in deepest conversation, it's a kind of sacred whispering or murmur, the most intimate secret I shall not speak of again, and the sound of softly falling rain and how one who loves cannot calculate as Kierkegaard once wrote or groaned maybe more accurately stated or expressed, and then, oh, yes, big props and capital letters to Brother Lawrence who once said, "I have need to busy my heart with quietude"—and thus am I always off to another, ever more obscure trout stream with the fumes of a hangover and three-day beard and delirious joy in my heart unmatched in the annals of middle age, and how can it be that we sometimes live long enough to one day see the second doorway of childhood opening in a meadow or a forest and watering the flowers again in the early morning, with bunnies abounding near the peonies who are so lush in their abundance they cannot even hold up their skull-sized blossoms, and then I hear William's voice again saying "God loves you so dearly that nothing you are can stay but all the time you keep going away, away," in his poem "Grandmother Watching At Her Window," which I have heard so many times with Tina over the years on a CD that his voice is somehow a part of our fathomless love that keeps deepening every hour, every second, every minute, and now brushing the ferns as I walk on the trail with my fingertips under the vast canopy of white pines and cedars so fernfully, fernfully, I feel or somehow gloriously infer that this is what we must have been made for after all, to celebrate everything just because it is, as Milosz once wrote, and somehow this brief touching of the ferns is a tiny but no less sacred part of all of it, walking this path of staggering beauty that never ends.

***

The Good Samaritan
by Duane Anderson

It was my first night out of town,
all alone, waiting for a table to free up
to eat my evening meal.
First, seated at a table for six,
then moved to a table for four as there
was nothing available for a party of one.

I sat there with the other three chairs to keep me company,
with names of Nobody, Zilch, and Zero.
Maybe I should have gone to a place less crowded,
where the food might not have been as tasty,
but at least, I would not have occupied a table in such short supply.
I stayed, ate, until my appetite has been satisfied,

then waited for my server to present me with the bill,
one, that never came, a bill I found out had already been paid.
I looked around, looking for my saint,
but I did not see anyone else smiling besides myself.
I had been blessed, receiving an affirmation
that there are still some things going right in this world.

Scalding Communion
by Sharisa Aidukaitis

scalding communion
mugs steaming around new words
midwife to friendship

Throne of Alone

by Kaylee Baucom

Four days until forty
And it's a gift to be alone
No man around to sour my mood
No woman about to judge my ways
No human beings to point out the stumbles I've made walking through the maize

The real treasure is to be on one's own
(Gold souls can only purify when alone)
It's natural to want someone here
But here is too near when they're whispering in your ear

No man about to persuade my mind
No woman around to treat me unkind
The gift was given once I shed what I'd outgrown
To live in my forty crown
On my Throne of Alone

"but I did not see anyone else
smiling besides myself.
I had been blessed, receiving an
affirmation
that there are still some things
going right in this world."

~ Duane Anderson

Enjoy the Silence
by Ella Piazzi

Growing up as a child, I always believed that by the age of 42 and 1/6, I would have had my life in order. I would have reached all the milestones that I have been taught were 'fundamental' to becoming a person, and my days would be a long string of age-appropriate, military-precision-organised activities that made me an adult.

At the age of 42 and 1/6, I accomplished a bunch of botched milestones, I still enjoy non-age-appropriate activities, like watching anime or drawing, my diary is organised using a scattergun approach and conversations in my head with my childhood trauma are a daily essential.

Trauma is like caging a tree; it will grow a weird shape, but it will still be a tree. Unlike trees, though, I have feelings and mood swings. Some days are good, while other days, like today, I feel a waste of time, space and oxygen.

Because you always had to be different.

If I could choose to be anything, I wouldn't choose to be me.

While I deal with this insane dose of self-loathing, I also have to provide for myself. If you decide to be the black sheep, don't expect any help. You don't deserve it. Get yourself a job, pay taxes, give up your seat if someone needs it, even if you are exhausted.

You could have had an office job and a car, if you'd stayed here and followed the path so many of us took before you.

I never wanted an office job or a car, and even less I wanted to follow the path so many took before me *because it's not mine.*

What do you want to do, then?

I want to be a writer. In the little iron cage that doubled as bedroom and whole world, I believed that writers were these mystical creatures that spent their days writing the stories they had in their heads, creating beautiful worlds in solitude, then touring the wide world presenting their amazing books.

That's what a better life looks like?

To me, yes. That's a life I would enjoy.

Now I know that being a writer is not just that. It's not even possible like that anymore. You have deadlines and not every single thing you write will be published – more likely, most of the things you write *won't* be published. Plus, in modern times it's impossible to survive just being a writer. Unless you're really – and I mean REALLY – lucky and you only produce bestseller after bestseller.

You'll never make it then. Why don't you stop?

I need a reason to get up from bed every morning and not throwing myself under a bus. I need to know that I tried, that I did all I could. I just need to make it. I just... Please...

Today is definitely not a good day.

The clock on my phone says it's 17:54. Time to get ready.

You are ridiculous.

Ok, fine. There are times when I feel out of place. But when I started, and I was placed in the 'adults' group, I expected people aged 30+.

Instead, you are mixing yourself with teenagers. Some of them could be your children.

And yet, in Taekwondo terms, they are my seniors.

Of course. Because they are skinnier, faster and better than you.

It takes time, and the older you are, the longer it will take you. But as usual, you are missing the point.

You are missing the point. You should have done it when you were younger. Now it's not the time anymore.

Would you have let me?

Of course not. It's violent and for men, and you can get injured.

That also encompasses 85% of my daily activities. I don't see you stopping me.

I blink, once, twice. Three times. The world around me resurfaces one piece at a time. The living room, with its soft lighting, the radio playing rock anthems, my manga collections, the to-be-read piles of books on the floor by the bookshelf, the potted plant I was gifted on my last birthday and the drying rack opened in front of the heater. My wife is in the kitchen prepping something – I think it's broccoli by the sound of it – and the washing machine is rinsing. Inside my head is the umpteenth boxing match I will lose with my mother's voice, but around me is just an ordinary Thursday night.

My phone says it's 18:01. I have lost another four minutes of my life fighting ghosts I will never kill.

You never learn.

No. I am a hopeless optimist.

First, I fix my knee braces – a must after my double knee injury,

you hurt yourself because you are fat

then I wear my dobok, which makes me look like a sack of potatoes,

you were way thinner when I put you on a diet

fill up my water bottle and check my duffle: kick-pad, belt, keys, asthma inhaler. There are times when the weight on my chest is actual asthma and not anxiety.

"I'm ready!" I shout to the wife, who is now moving from one room to another, taking care of the many menial little things that constitute adult life: cook this, put that away, clean this, bin that.

"Have fun throwing kicks with the other psychopaths![1] Don't get too injured and don't hurt anyone."

"I'll do my best," I say, kissing her goodbye before walking down the stairs.

I know I am repeating myself, but you are ridiculous.

Let's analyse the matter with some objectivity: on a scale from 1 to 10, my present skills are at a solid 4 and 1/2. Power comes with practice, and I am working hard on balance and coordination.

You are too old for these things.

I put my headphones on and press play on one of my heavy metal playlists, then walk to the platform and wait for my train. There are a lot of people waiting with me, occupied in different activities: chatting with their travel companion, talking on the phone, or simply listening to music, their work passes still hanging around their neck. A corner of my mind registers how they all look like respectable people, busy in respectable and age-appropriate activities.

Don't worry. They've already noticed you, because your jacket is too tight around your waist and you're dressed like an idiot.

I tighten my grip on my bag strap and glance at the departure board. I flex my legs and bounce from one foot to the other. Two more minutes. I check my phone, then look at the big stretch of sky in front of me, almost completely dark. It's incredible how days have shortened in such little time. When the train arrives, I squeeze into a corner, right beside the doors, trying to ignore the claustrophobia that is teaming up with the anxiety. When I can't take it any

---

"It's adrenaline and fear and excitement, the power and friendship and camaraderie, the weight of history and tradition and the lightness of taking silly selfies with your mates."

---

longer, I mentally review the kicks I have learnt so far, thinking about where my supporting foot is supposed to be, focusing on the position of my core, of my arms, of my hands.

It's only six stops to Dalston Kingsland, but it
seems longer.

When I arrive, I bolt, but I'm stuck in a mud-like river of humans moving towards the exit in a chaotic and yet slow way. I am grateful for the fresh air.

What's this bad smell?

The Turkish restaurants and kebab shops on the high street are in full swing, their yellow lights dotting the darkness like micro suns, with people going in and out as if they were playing musical chairs. Cars are lining up the street, with the sporadic bus stuck in between them, red lights, yellow lights, white lights, a blue one from an emergency service as well.

Of course, you have asthma; look where you live.

Delivery drivers are moving swiftly left, right and centre on their e-bikes and security guards are scattered around in their hi-vis jackets.

How can you like a place like this? It's pro-

[1] My wife said it to me one Spring Thursday night at the beginning to this year. It became our inside joke.

I am close. Finally. I smell the reassuring sweetness of the cleaning chemical and air freshener that Master Wayne uses, and I fill up my lungs, my body and my mind with it.

Then I feel it.

The itch.

It starts like pins and needles, then grows. My heart beats slightly faster, my walk is slightly quicker, my breath is slightly better, my smile is slightly bigger. It's like pressing a long series of buttons, switching something off and switching something else on. It's adrenaline and fear and excitement, the power and friendship and camaraderie, the weight of history and tradition and the lightness of taking silly selfies with your mates. It's the knowledge of entering the dojang as one person and leaving it as a person 1% better than before.

A deep breath and down I go, along the stairs that lead to a long and narrow basement covered in black and white mats. It's interchange time, so I wiggle my body and my huge bag to go in while the juniors are going out. First of all, I take off my shoes and socks – we train barefoot – then bow, and last, I enter. There isn't a proper door, just the frame in the wall, but passing that threshold is like being in the middle of a 2000-year-old crossroads. Taekwondo started as a fighting and defensive technique for those who didn't have or couldn't obtain weapons, and it's now a form of self-defence and a competitive sport, but its origins of raw energy and spirituality are still there, so thick that they are almost tangible.

I get my pad and my water and put them in a corner, before doing my belt in front of the mirror – there is a specific way to do it. Then I smile at my reflection: I am no longer a sack of potatoes.

My mates come in, and we share hugs and handshakes and bows, we throw banter and show off turning kicks and sidekicks, already choosing sparring partners for later.

At 7 pm sharp, Master Wayne opens his office door and the air fizzles. He is a short man, with a warm smile and reassuring manners, but underneath the Splinter aura, there is a lethal nerve and many years of study and practice. I would never spar with him. And not because he is my Master.

"Fall in!" he calls. "Cha Ryut!" *THWACK!* "Kyung Ye!" fhss "Go, go, GO!"

A simple string of commands: stand at attention, bow, start running. Once we've warmed up, we proceed with a series of stretching exercises and kick combinations before we couple up to practice. Soon our legs become heavy, our muscles burn and big drops of sweat roll from unexpected places.

"Have a minute rest," says Master Wayne after the last buzzer.

"Thank you, Sir," comes the unanimous response. Right now, we are one. The dojang is where everything begins and ends. I smile. I feel happy. I am *alive.*

"Fall back in! This is not summer camp!"

We start again, the combinations of kicks become more demanding, we grow tired, yet no one slows down. Right now, I have full control over my motions; my body is a wonderful machine that can balance on one foot and hit with the other leg, my mind is clear, my lungs are open and pumping air. I can twist and block and attack with precision and control. I feel good.

I feel

GREAT.

The buzzer goes off one more time and the order comes.

"Gear up!"

Show time! On Thursdays, we spar. It sounds like a grandiose thing – it is, for us – but from the

"You alone are the judge of your worth, and your goal is to discover infinite worth in yourself, no matter what anyone else thinks."

~ Deepak Chopra

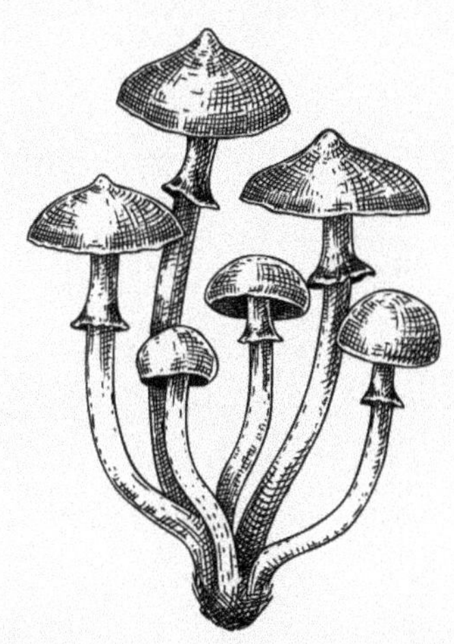

outside, we probably look like a bunch of fanatics kicking each other. But unless we wear body armour, shin and head guards, we can't touch each other, not even in a playful way.

When the buzzer goes off, my opponent is the only thing that exists. I block a side kick with my right arm and respond with a turning kick using my right leg, then I go for a push kick aimed at the core, but I am faced with a powerful spinning kick that throws me off balance. I am attacked with a double turning kick that I block only thanks to muscle memory, then I try a counterattack that also relies on muscle memory. I hold the core the best I can, keep my guard up and breathe. As my partner is now far, I try a jumping back kick. And I execute it. I didn't jump much, and it wasn't so powerful, but it landed where it had to. I block a side kick with my leg, throw a reverse punch, then I get ready for a back kick when the buzzer goes off.

I am short of breath, and I am pretty sure I will have a bruise on my arm tomorrow, but there will be time for this. Later. Now I have two more rounds ahead of me. I grow tired, and I become sloppier, but I can't stop. I want more.

I *need* more.

The last buzzer goes off.

"You worked so hard tonight that you deserve a reward!"

"Thank you, Sir!"

And down we go, for push-ups and sit-ups and a lot of grunting. And last, we recite the tenets of Taekwondo.

1. courtesy.
2. integrity.
3. perseverance.
4. self-control.
5. indomitable spirit.

We bow, one last time, then I bow again when I exit the dojang. Every joint, every muscle ache, every nerve is still buzzing. I am lighter, better, happier, stronger, than I was one hour ago. I practised my kicks, and I executed a couple very well. For one hour, I wasn't my childhood trauma. For a few more hours, I won't fight any voice in my head, and I won't be a waste of time, space and oxygen, but an indestructible warrior that is not afraid of shit.

I look at the sky above my head, dark and with no stars, and I smile. There will come a time when I'll be leaving the dojang and the sky will be blue, and the sun will still be in the sky.

I reach the station, wait for my train on a now-empty platform and board. No more than a handful of people are sitting around me. I fired a text to the wife and smiled, tired but blissful.

Finally enjoying a minute of well-deserved silence.

***

I Enjoy My Third Self...
by Sam Barbee

A poet scans morning, petitions
the muse for a seamless draft.

Spent years dreaming, other nights an insomniac—
those grains spilled through the hourglass already:

My sleepy eyes measure meter, granular
seconds and rhyme ooze tedious lines.

Both dawn and dusk grind me, arguing
verb tenses. I take a time out to vacuum...

and suck up a few gems from opened joints
in the hardwood floor. Scribble them...

Some animal instinct roars, roused.
I give the muse a kiss on the cheek.

Another day came... now ether. All call
at the corner tavern... I buy the next round.

The Quarterpipe's Query

by Kiyoshi Hirawa

I was spinning in the air, ambition outpacing ability, when my headlamp slipped off and I free-fell into darkness. Though I've read and written many metaphors, that was the first one I'd ever *felt*, and I feared and savored the sensation.

I shouldn't have even been there, shouldn't have been flailing in the murk, the headlamp bouncing away and illuminating everything but the way down. Instead, I should've been dropping a gun into a holster and pinning a badge over my heart. But two years prior, I was wrongfully terminated by my police department after I began speaking out about sexual misconduct. At that moment, I should've been piercing – not plummeting through – the darkness, protecting the neighborhoods I once prowled as a teen.

When you're exiled for telling the truth by a profession that purportedly seeks truth at all costs, you acquire a special kind of corrosive gloom, a perpetual twilight. And while therapy, family, and friends can help, ultimately, you're on your own to seek a new dawn. You need a new path of light, not just a diversion or hobby, but a pursuit of joy that creates a new part of you independent of every past root.

Like the pursuit of a Fakie 720 halfway through your fifth decade.

*

I was thinking about professional athlete Fabiola da Silva as I fell. This was really all her fault. Fabiola is exactly my age, and that's precisely where the similarities end. I could do a bit here, describe her and then contrast her attributes with some humorous self-deprecation, but that feels a little cavalier towards the woman crowned Queen of the Vert Ramp. So, I'll just drop her bio, and you can assume the opposite of every adjective for me. Fabiola is a legendary Brazilian aggressive inline skater of such prolonged dominance that the Aggressive Skaters Association changed the rules to allow her to compete against the men in vert ramp competitions. As transcendent as Simone Biles or Michaela Shiffrin or Serena Williams are, nobody's changing the rules so they can compete against men.

I first watched Fabiola compete in the 1996 X games in Rhode Island, and I could not believe what I was watching. The vert ramp (picture an elongated U whose walls are fourteen feet high) was contending with every skater, tolerating a trick or combination or a big air, then sabotaging their run and issuing stern reminders about gravity and mortality. And then Fabiola dropped in. It was as if the vert ramp surrendered and became a spectator, fan-girling over a seventeen-year-old who would later regularly record top ten finishes in male competitions. It was the first time that I didn't just admire a professional athlete, I wanted to *be* like that athlete.

Except, as I watched her vault and backflip like Athena come down to Newport, I thought, *I could never do that.*

And so, I didn't.

> "I felt strangely eager to try again rather than drive home. Each attempt felt like an answer to the questions echoing off the skatepark's ramps and jump boxes…"

After my police department exiled me, I felt like my identity had crashed to earth, the various parts strewn across fields and forests like a downed satellite. My initial instinct was to frantically recover and reassemble as many parts as possible.

And then one day, Fabiola showed up in my suggested YouTube feed, and I realized, stunned, that she wasn't just still skating, she was still *competing*. After watching a few videos, I halted my search for all the exploded parts of my identity and began contemplating what new parts I might construct. The *what if* questions started lurking and could not be chased.

A week later, I started shopping online for skates. I recalled a line from Pablo Neruda's "Poetry": "*…something started in my soul, fever or forgotten wings.*"

Naturally, I wanted a pair of Fabiola's signature blades, but the specs advised the boot was designed for narrower feet, yet another way that Fabiola and I differed. There was no way I could cram my toad feet into her skates, so I reluctantly broadened my search and found a pair amenable to vert ramps and also street skating (think curbs, railings, and benches). They were Nico Auroux's signature skates, a renowned French skater whose name means *bright victory*. When you're that deep in the pit, any coincidence becomes a rope, so I traced and measured my feet on a piece of paper, crossed my fingers about the sizing, and clicked "purchase."

*

Falling is an inherent part of aggressive inlining. You blade, you'll bite it, eventually. There's nothing terribly philosophical about this, it's just the inevitability of more speed and less friction. For skaters, the pride of success is always built on the pain of failure. Even knowing this, however, I hadn't planned on so deeply enjoying failure.

My first session at the local skatepark was a low-light reel of scraped knuckles, bruised hips, and sore shoulders. I started showing up to work with bandaged elbows. I developed scars where I'd thought about getting tattoos.

I declined to volunteer explanations to any inquiring gazes. My new hobby was like a new relationship. I wanted to keep it private and protected for as long as possible, so I bought better equipment, knee pads and elbow pads, as well as a pair of padded shorts.

I continued to fall often and fall hard, yet each time, I felt strangely eager to try again rather than drive home. Each attempt felt like an answer to the questions echoing off the skatepark's ramps and jump boxes – the same queries demanded by any hobby worth its salt: *what are you willing to sacrifice, how much are you willing to commit, how much do you trust yourself, and how will you respond to adversity?*

The concrete quarterpipe that had taken its pound of flesh from me asked these same questions, yet the replies were much more visceral. The answers were also much more incomplete. I knew that I was sacrificing safety and possibly a pain-free week. I knew that each run, each trick, demanded complete commitment (every skating video preaches, "You have to commit," with the unspoken warning that partial commitment is the greatest danger of all). I also knew that trusting myself was my biggest weakness because I lacked experience, and in turn, confidence. And the bone-bruises and shredded elbows told me everything I needed to know about adversity.

But these questions and answers felt lacking, and I didn't know why until I took an unexpected pilgrimage while out of town at a conference.

*

The open road naturally invites existential questions. When you're the only person in the car, however, and the drive is eight hours long and the destination is a conference on artificial intelligence, the mind finds some strange trails. Many people daydream about their passions, and as I drove, I visualized different tricks at different skate parks. Yet each daydream was interrupted by a question I'd been ignoring ever since my skates arrived six months earlier: *why*? As in, why was I doing this? This hobby was costing money, not earning it, and the potential for injury grew with each new trick, but I couldn't stop.

I was working toward a specific trick, something called a Fakie 720. This trick involves skating backwards up a vert ramp, completing two full 360s, and then descending the vert ramp, also backwards. I had no problem flying backwards up the ramp, but I was struggling to spin. Just skating backwards in a loop made me dizzy, and my lack of aerial awareness was becoming a major hurdle. I felt like Thomas Edison when he insisted that he never failed at inventing the light bulb, he just discovered thousands of ways not to make one. I was fast approaching the discovery of at least one hundred ways to crash and not land this trick. And I didn't even know why I was pursuing it.

The first day of the conference, after the day's events ended, I dropped by an indoor skatepark described by its online reviews as nothing short of a religious experience. I stepped inside the twenty-thousand-square-foot warehouse, and two things became immediately apparent.

First, based on the demographics and abilities of the skaters alone, I did not belong there, especially being the only one on inline skates.

And second, no one said a word about it. No smirks, no sidelong glances, no under the breath comments. I was accepted as just another denizen of the skatepark ecosystem. People yelled, "Board!" to warn of out-of-control skateboards, apologized for near-collisions, and answered questions without a trace of condescension. It was the most welcoming place I've ever been.

After a couple of hours, I sat on a bench and watched skaters shred the bowl, a six-foot high semi-circle that flowed down into a larger circle with walls approaching ten feet. There were men and women of all ages and aptitudes. I saw a six-year-old crash on the smaller bowl, shrug, then belly-flop and slide down into the larger bowl on his pads as his dad laughed from the ledge. As each skater dropped in, I pondered why they skated, what their reason was, since I hadn't discerned mine.

If God speaks in cathedrals, then Fabiola must speak in skateparks because I heard a Brazilian-accented and mildly exasperated voice gently whisper, "If you need a reason to skate, then maybe you shouldn't be wearing those blades."

It was the absolution I did not know I'd been seeking, permission to pursue something for no other reason than it brought me the bliss I'd found so elusive. Whenever I recount this skatepark epiphany, I like to joke, "I came for the healing – I stayed for the joy." Whatever guilt or misgivings I'd been carrying, I left it all on that bench overlooking the bowl as I dropped in and carved out one of the smoothest runs of my short skating career.

*

There's an old psychologist joke that goes something like this.

"Happiness," mused the psychologist, "is the pursuit of something, not actually catching it."

"Have you ever," replied the patient, "chased the last bus of the evening in the pouring rain?"

Both people are right. The nature of the pursuit is just as important as the quarry, and vice versa. Landing the Fakie 720 would be momentous, but only as long as it's one of many points on an ever-evolving trajectory of joy. And if the pursuit of this or any other trick becomes miserable, it's time to get out of the rain. There are other ways home, even if we have to invent them.

Like blading in the dark.

That's how I learned to skate. I was too embarrassed to practice in front of anyone, so I waited until the skatepark was abandoned and dark to venture onto the quarterpipes and jump boxes, headlamp strapped to my helmet. My first trick, a frontside grind where I skated up and slid across the coping atop the ramp, was witnessed by three pine trees and a fox. Frequently, joy is a contagion or vector, insisting on spreading out from its source. I would suggest that another equally potent form of joy exists, the kind that detonates within private triumph and remains an enduring source of secret energy and strength.

That night, under a full moon in October, I was warming up on the quarterpipe and jump boxes. No tricks, just limbering up after sitting all day at work. During a very basic jump, my headlamp snapped off, and there was nothing but moonlight above and darkness below as I hung in mid-air.

Maybe it was the endless inline skating videos I'd watched. Or the countless crashes over the last many months. Or the feeling that'd been falling for the last two years, and I was weary of flailing in the dark. Or maybe it was just Fabiola's voice in my ear, whispering, *Why?*

Whatever the case, I relaxed, committed to my position, and trusting myself, felt for the concrete. I landed firmly, wheels humming, and glided to a stop in the shadows.

It was still dark, but I had my skates and my scars, and the quarterpipe's query had been answered.

***

Inner Peace
by Noor Safaa

Simple sneaking, waiting glee
Comes and goes around me.
It holds my hands so tightly,
Wants me to write, to breathe,
Wants me to turn my thoughts off.
Soft lights on, papers scattered, ink drops.

Sun rays gently, softly cross
The spaces of hope in my windows.
Turn the radio on and on—
Things happen before they are done.
A day comes, another goes,
All that's left are laughter echoes.

Take a photo of your favourite view,
While family gathers around you.
Turn the camera to the other side—
Each one's sadness hides.

The sound of healing becomes loud
Once your inner peace is found.

DECEMBER, 2025 // ISSUE 04

Thorn & Bloom

Radical Joy We Cultivate

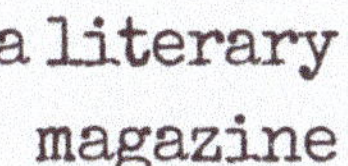

Thank you to everyone who submitted their work and entrusted us with their words—we are honoured to hold space for your voices, and delighted to share your stories with others.

A special heartfelt thank you to Olivia Ho for taking the time to answer my questions. It is always a joy to read her insights into literature and see how she will match her love of vintage fashion with her passion for reading. And I must say, it is pure delight to know there are people out there who value the art and importance of books. Thank you for showing others how joyful reading can be.

CONTACT INFO:

www.redrosethorns.com
/
contact@redrosethorns.com
/
@redrosethorns

www.ingramcontent.com/pod-product-compliance
Lightning Source LLC
Chambersburg PA
CBHW041210100726
47911CB00017B/909